Come Near at your Peril:

A Visitor's Guide to the Island of Newfoundland
New Edition

by
Patrick O'Flaherty

BREAKWATER

Breakwater
100 Water Street
P.O. Box 2188
St. John's, NF.
A1C 6E6

Cover Photo: *Crawley's Cove, Nfld.*
Clyde Rose

Canadian Cataloguing in Publication Data

O'Flaherty, Patrick, 1939-

  Come near at your peril

  ISBN 1-55081-100-2

1. Newfoundland — Guidebooks. I. Title.

FC2167.5.045 1994   917.1804'4   C94-950087-9
F1122.045 1994

Contents

Preface

This is a personal, unauthorized guidebook to many of the places I have visited in Newfoundland. The idea to write such a work came to me some years ago in a self-service restaurant in Florence, Italy, when I was obliged to pay a service charge before taking my dish of gummy-looking food to a dirty table. "Someone should have warned me about things like this," I said to myself. This book is the kind I wanted to have then—full of frank advice and warnings, a book by someone on the visitor's side.

Many communities are left out of this guide. Sorry about that. I either visited them and didn't feel like writing about them, or else I didn't visit them. Despite having knocked around the island for about thirty years, I confess there are still quite a few places on it I haven't seen.

The book moves from west to east. I assume the visitor arrives via the Marine Atlantic ferry at Port aux Basques on the southwest corner and proceeds to drive across the island, taking various detours on the way, departing on the ferry from Argentia in Placentia Bay.

I have confined myself in this work to insular Newfoundland. Islands off the coast of Newfoundland will be featured in my book, *Newfoundland's Offshore Islands: A Guide.*

I want to thank the following for help on specific points: Joe Brazil, Dave Coffin, Don Hustins, Calvin Yates, Chris Brown, Peter Scott, Wayne Benoit, Carl Wheaton, Doug Ballam, Gordon Handcock, Ben Dunne, Ken Curnew, Louise Daley, and especially Marjorie Doyle, my companion on many of the jaunts described here, who read the manuscript and made numerous valuable suggestions.

In this second edition I have, again with Marjorie Doyle's substantial help, updated, deleted, and added, where appropriate.

February 7, 1994.

Introduction

One classic description of Newfoundland, often quoted by writers unable to better it, was R.T.S. Lowell's: "The huge island ... stands, with its sheer, beetling cliffs, out of the ocean, a monstrous mass of rock and gravel, almost without soil, like a strange thing from the bottom of the great deep, lifted up, suddenly, into sunshine and storm, but belonging to the watery darkness out of which it has been reared; the eye, accustomed to richer and softer scenes, finds something of a strange and almost startling beauty in its bold, hard outlines, cut out on every side, against the sky."

Thus Lowell, an American missionary writing in the 1840s. His unsentimental words capture much about Newfoundland: its primitive, northern character, unpredictable climate, harsh outlines; and two of its three essential elements—rock and water. (The third being the woods and scrub: where Lowell lived, these were typically low-lying conifers, alders, and gorsy thicket; tough, clinging, "a stinted growth," as he wrote, "slow-growing in long years.") But it has to be kept in mind that, gifted as he was, Lowell knew only the Avalon Peninsula; perhaps he also saw the southern coastline a few times from a ship. He knew little or nothing of the island's forested interior or its west and north coasts. There are parts of the island that do not fit his description, parts where, had he visited them, he would have felt almost as if he were in another world. Many notes are sounded in Newfoundland; he heard one.

Yet it was and is the dominant one. Lowell's description is something every visitor to the island should know, for, knowing it, he or she would not then ask of the place what it cannot give. Newfoundland is a primeval and still relatively unspoiled corner of the North American continent. In its own way, it is beautiful and appealing; but it can be more appalling than appealing. The weather is unsettled: cold, foggy, rainy, windy, and sometimes sunny. A quick change of wind can turn a warm day cold and drizzly. You can get a week or more of awful weather in July, August, and September, the good months. In 1991, it snowed in June, there was a frost warning on August 25, there were still icebergs in Notre Dame Bay in early September, and it snowed again in October. In 1992, it snowed on July 3. This is not to say it never gets hot; you can get a bad sunburn if you think that, especially if you go out on the salt water for a few hours when the sun is shining.

Nor is the weather the only thing that might put you off. The terrain is rugged and not to everyone's taste. Most graphic artists tend to like it—Rockwell Kent, Frederic Edwin Church, Albert Cloutier, and many others have been inspired by what Ann Meredith Barry calls its "biblical, elemental quality; no gussying up, no prettying over"—but at least one painter, the gifted, contrary Peter Bell, saw it differently. He didn't even like the trees, which he thought spiky and silly-looking. Another observer, put off by the rocks and bogs, said: "So much of Newfoundland looks as though it has lain for an epoch under an ice cap."

The salt water is so cold that along the northeast coast only the foolhardy dare take a summer swim in it. Toughened youngsters in swimsuits are sometimes seen leaping off wharves; a few seconds later, they crawl out of the water, skin shivering, teeth chattering.

Inland, mosquitoes are often a nuisance, as are deer flies and sand flies. Some people always carry flydope in their pockets and take sturdy windbreakers on summer picnics. These are wise people.

There are settlements in the interior of Newfoundland, and even two important towns (Gander and Grand Falls). But the central portions of the island are mostly wilderness—though much of it has been either ravaged by the pulp and paper companies, which have operated here since early in the 20th century, or flooded by the hydro authority. Human life tends to be carried on around the edges of this island, in hundreds of communities of assorted sizes, the biggest of which is St. John's, the capital. The Trans-Canada Highway from Port aux Basques to St. John's stays mostly inland; spinning off from it, like spiralling threads of thin kelp from a central stalk, are various roads, often optimistically termed highways, which in turn lead to other roads, which lead to the outlying places where people fish, cut wood, or farm for a living, or just live. Visitors have to get off the TCH onto these smaller highways, swim in the ponds and brooks, sit on the headlands, smell the salt air, feel the fog on their faces, walk on the barrens and marshes, stop off at small communities, and meet the people, in order to experience the true gritty flavor of Newfoundland. You cannot say you know Newfoundland until you have done some or all of these things.

This mention of highways has a modern ring: but it is important to note that, from the air, Newfoundland often seems uninhabited; indeed, the mixture of marsh, skinny ponds, and scrub spruce that you see below as you fly east towards the Avalon Peninsula makes it look uninhabit*able*. The island has just over half a million inhabitants, yet it has sent emigrants to the U.S., every province of Canada, and farther afield. Coming here was one thing; staying here, another. As novelist Margaret Duley wrote, "One has to be tough to be a resident." And there are many places where the thought occurs that even a population of half a million has had little impact on the terrain. The weather forces people indoors, and you can drive through communities in the fog, or even not in the fog, and think them ghost towns. Men and women have carved up southern Ontario into squares and the sides of the St. Lawrence in Quebec into narrow rectangles; they have not carved Newfoundland up, though they have scraped at it, dug into it, and lived off it long enough to make an impression. But it is hard to change the look of a rock.

External nature on this island is more a force to be confronted than a vista to be enjoyed. It is a place where man and woman must perforce develop the virtue of humility, and be content to inhabit what the writer Norman Duncan called "a thin, jagged strip, between a wilderness of scrawny shrubs and the sea's fretful expanse."

It is proper to state right away what the island offers the occasional visitor and tourist. It offers what Duley, quoting Keats, called a "cold pastoral." It is a good venue for wilderness experience: camping, backpacking, canoeing, hiking, bird-watching, berry-picking, beachcombing, iceberg watching, whale-watching, photography, film-making, fishing, sailing, hunting, or just looking. Remember the pleasures of just looking! Newfoundland is a rock surrounded by very cold salt water; accordingly, if you like to do things on salt water, or even (should you be a scuba-diver or a kayaker) *in* salt water, you have found your spot. Ditto, fresh water; there are ponds, lakes, rivers, brooks, and gullies everywhere. If you happen to be eremetic by inclination and enjoy visiting abandoned offshore islands, your wishes can readily be satisfied. A glance at Bonavista Bay on the map, or at other bays, will show what a proliferation of islands awaits you. Wilderness is never far away in Newfoundland; therefore, if the wilds and its flora and fauna and solitudes are what interests you, again you may well be merry during your stay. Should you be one of those rare creatures who enjoy blustery weather, even in July and August, this "great wedge of rock, tip-tilted against a continent, seemingly sliced off from it by a sardonic nature"—as novelist Percy Janes describes it—may well turn out to be your Brigadoon.

But if you want Anne of Green Gables greenery, then go to Cavendish in Prince Edward Island. PEI is a pretty little island. Newfoundland is not a pretty little island.

A few more words of caution. Newfoundland has not got the level of prosperity enjoyed by many other parts of North America, but this doesn't mean the people don't hanker for it. They do hanker for it. And why shouldn't they? We now have, in certain places, a bustling "tourist industry" which is only too happy to sell you services, trinkets, food, trips, and anything else you need or desire. I hate the phrase "tourist industry," because what it amounts to, here as elsewhere, is turning an innocent custom—visiting another province or country—into a commercial enterprise whose intent is to squeeze every cent out of travellers. Places which emphasize a tourist "industry" normally have no other legitimate industries to rely on. But there it is: a business it has become. Much of this business here is done in a thoroughly competent and professional way: e.g., the outfitting of hunters and guiding of salmon fishermen, certain wilderness and harbor tours operating out of St. John's and other centers, many motels, hotels, restaurants, gift shops, etc. Some of it, however, is makeshift and sloppy. In their hurry to concoct a

"Newfoundland custom" that they can impose on unwary travellers, a few hucksters have even invented "traditional" ceremonies such as the hateful "Screech-In" or the even more repulsive "Kissing-The-Cod," both of which should of course be avoided in case you catch trench mouth.

By contrast, many communities make no pretense whatever of appealing to tourists, and you will find few of what you might consider normal visitors' amenities in them. You will usually find a post office and gas tank. There is no shortage of churches, should you need one of those. Also, there will be a general store of some kind: it may be termed a "convenience," a "groc & conf," "Rita's," a "mini-mart," a "cash & carry," or even a "superette." These shops are often small, but do not disdain what they can offer. Food, rudimentary fishing and camping equipment, clothing, beer, cooking utensils, sewing gear, electrical appliances, batteries, film, tools, and much more can be found in these places. The excellent Co-Op Supermarket in Eastport, Bonavista Bay, sells food of course, but also books, cattle feed, and rubber boots. I once went into a small building called "Tim's Shop" looking for ice, and came out with, not just ice, but a can of tuna, a pair of sunglasses that have served me well for years, a tomahawk, six fly-hooks, and a six-pack of Molson's ale. If I'd wanted them, I could have also had a sack of flour, a chamber pot, and a video of "Bladerunner."

On first sight, the Newfoundland outport village may seem scraggly, elongated, and tarnished, with unpainted outbuildings, crumbling rock walls, untended wharves, fishing gear and wood junks piled every which way, clumps of alders or uncut tall grass and weeds along the road and between houses, etc. Car wrecks, let it be said, are not unknown in these parts, and you will not have to walk far on the paths behind some communities to find beer bottles, discarded refrigerators, and bags of trash. (The refrigerators you see in *front* of some homes are for garbage collection.) Do not be put off by this apparent contempt for prettiness. It is due partly to the fact that very little of what is termed town-planning has gone on here—indeed, municipal government itself is something new in most areas of the island—but also to the nature of the pursuits that have dominated the economy and shaped the society. Fishing is not a genteel business; neither is chopping down wood, hunting, or farming in the acid and rocky Newfoundland soil. The place offered people a rough living, and they responded somewhat in kind. One further point: the fishing economy of Newfoundland has been in decline for some years. There is now a federal government moratorium on the commercial cod and salmon fisheries all around the island, and the once abundant caplin are threatened. Certain communities have been harder hit than others. All this, of course, has had an effect on rural life.

However, many Newfoundland outports have more than a touch of postcard-cuteness. Woody Point in Bonne Bay comes to mind; as do King's Cove or, a little beyond it, Keels, Bonavista Bay; Maberly, southeast of Bonavista; Salvage, at the tip of the Eastport Peninsula; Little Harbour or Fairhaven, Placentia Bay; Port Kirwan, south of St. John's on route 10; Gooseberry Cove on the Cape Shore south of Placentia; Trinity, Trinity Bay; Moreton's Harbour in Notre Dame Bay; English Harbour West in Fortune Bay; or Upper Ferry and other places in the Codroy Valley. Nor are these the only ones. In books of photographs the exquisite side of Newfoundland is naturally emphasized, the sea is often calm, the boats lie at anchor near the stages, all is sunny and alluring and colorful. But photographers have tarted up rural scenery everywhere on earth. Those who have visited Ireland will know that man has left his smear even near the lakes of Killarney. On the roadside between the villages of Milhars and Vaour in an exquisite part of southeastern France there is a garbage dump. I have seen the stretch of

Scene at Upper Ferry, Codroy Valley

green effluent called the Tiber, smelled the Liffey in Dublin, on which not even a gull will pitch, and kept a safe distance from the Arno in Florence. By comparison, our lakes and streams have a certain distinct charm.

A few other landmarks of the contemporary Newfoundland outport need to be mentioned. You will see on the outskirts of these communities squat, barn-like structures, sometimes unpainted, set in a gravel pit, and called "lounges." These are taverns; too often, they are foul-smelling places, dark, dismal, to be avoided by the sensible visitor who wishes to stay out of trouble. On Saturday nights they sometimes feature loud, vulgar music. The only buildings somewhat resembling these in shape in Newfoundland are schools. Very little money has been invested in architecture or landscaping by school boards in Newfoundland, with the result that children are being educated in buildings that you could at times mistake for abatoirs or the aforementioned beer-parlours. A third feature of the rural scene that might strike you as odd is the so-called "playground." These playgrounds were built in recent decades through "make-work" grants given by the federal government in an effort to reduce the official unemployment rate. Though many have equipment of the kind that you might find in Primrose Hill, London, or Central Park, they tend to be overgrown with nettles, dilapidated, and, since there is ample room for children to play in surrounding beaches and barrens, empty. You may also note abandoned hockey rinks, softball diamonds, and outdoor swimming pools in or near outports. Or even elaborate "recreation centres." Uncle Ottawa built those too. Newfoundland, I venture to say, has more softball diamonds and playgrounds per capita than any other part of the country.

I use the word "outport" to refer to any small village, or big village for that matter, outside the major towns. It is generally thought that the "Newfoundland way of life" or "Newfoundland culture" may be best experienced in these places. There is much to be said for this view. Just as in Ireland, where you must go west to Connaught and south to the ring of Kerry to breathe the true essence, so in Newfoundland you have to tackle the Great Northern Peninsula, New World Island, and the Cape Shore. But there are cities and towns as well; these are not to be neglected. I do not emphasize them much in the subsequent pages, because they offer what many mid-size Canadian towns offer: offices, libraries, hospitals, supermarkets, museums, fast food chains, and laundromats (though not always). Much as I like Stephenville, Clarenville, Baie Verte, Lewisporte, Botwood, Twillingate, and Marystown, I would not want to spend a two-week holiday in one of them, or for that matter in any other Newfoundland town, except St. John's (in summer and fall) and Corner Brook (in winter especially, for the skiing). An essential component of a Newfoundland holiday, to me, is highway travel.

History

Let me level with you on the historical attractions of Newfoundland. If you like castles, cathedrals, old walled cities on hills, and other ancient relics, then a day's visit to one village in France will likely stand you in better stead than a decade in Newfoundland. (Or a decade in Canada, for that matter.) Permanent European settlement in Newfoundland dates from the 17th century: no big deal. Of course, there was history before then—in fact, Newfoundland was settled from Labrador around 3000 B.C. by the peoples belonging to what archaeologists term the

Maritime Archaic Tradition, probably the ancestors of the Beothuck Indians—but of the aboriginal inhabitants of the island hardly a trace remains. The last of the Beothucks, a woman named Shanadithit, died of tuberculosis in 1829. Scholars have an imperfect grasp of even the language the Beothucks spoke. The Micmacs, whose descendants inhabit the Conne River region of the south coast, were, according to the best information I can obtain, latecomers to Newfoundland, as were the English, French, Irish, and other races. (I have to add here that the Micmacs themselves claim to be aboriginal people on the island.)

The first Europeans to find Newfoundland came in "poor, crazy, open row boats." So, at any rate, the Viking longboats, now highly regarded by Norwegian environmentalists, were described by historian and judge D.W. Prowse in his delightful *Newfoundland Guide Book* of 1905. The Vikings came to Newfoundland around 1000 A.D. and, evidently attracted by the open boglands and forests, planted a colony near the present settlement of L'Anse aux Meadows, close to the tip of the Great Northern Peninsula. The site was discovered and excavated in the 1960s; a reconstruction in authentic Norse fashion was carried out by Parks Canada. It was a small colony consisting of eight turf houses and a forge. How long it lasted remains unclear. Not very long. Had it endured, we might have had in Newfoundland such evidences of early European civilization as the Inquisition and the Black Death. If this site is indeed the "Vinland" (or Wineland) described in the old Norse *Sagas*, then one cause of its failure was the hostility shown to the settlers by the native peoples, who possibly had good reason to be hostile. These were the same Vikings who terrorized the coasts of England, Scotland, and Ireland in the 8th and 9th centuries. There is no good reason to suppose they turned into goodwill ambassadors in

Viking longboat replica near L'Anse aux Meadows, 1991.

northern Newfoundland. The L'Anse aux Meadows National Historic Park is the only authenticated Viking settlement in North America.

Local tourist brochures and government advertisements in glossy magazines tend to brag about Newfoundland as the "oldest British colony" and St. John's as "the oldest city in North America." They may even affirm that Newfoundland has "a history older than any other [place] in North America." These claims are spurious. Ireland was surely the oldest British colony (not that it is anything to boast about in any case), and the Mayas had cities in North America long before St. John's was anything but a deep crack in a rock. Leaving aside the ephemeral Viking settlement, the Europeans had a foothold elsewhere in North America as early as they had one here; indeed, earlier. Newfoundland punditry is full of claims of this kind. St. John's, for instance, in 1990 started calling itself the "City of Legends," although why it should deserve this title any more than, say, Barrie, Ontario, or Rimouski, Quebec, remains unclear.

People said to be authorities of some sort keep up the pretense that Newfoundland has had "400 years of settlement" or even 500. It is true that the first English colony on the island was planted in 1610, at Cupids, Conception Bay, by John Guy, ten years before the Puritans founded the Plymouth Colony. But neither this nor any subsequent attempt at colonization prior to 1661 was successful in the sense that they developed as the American colonies did—into robust, expanding communities. The few Europeans who survived here at the end of the 17th century were a leftover trickle from these early efforts at creating settlements. By the end of the 18th century, the population was still only around 30,000. In fact, it was not until very late in the day that the British government decided to allow Newfoundland to become a colony *comme les autres*; throughout the eighteenth century, Colonial Office policy was to keep the island as the preserve of migratory fishermen from the English west country. Britain didn't send out a year-round governor until 1816, and wouldn't grant a local legislature until 1832. (However, there has been a Supreme Court in Newfoundland since 1792.) There was no newspaper in St. John's until 1807. There was no legal right to own property in Newfoundland until 1819. My point is that institutions of government, the press, education, roads, communications, etc., lagged well behind those of the Americans or a closer colony such as Nova Scotia. Newfoundland is certainly not "as fresh as dulse," to quote E. J. Pratt, but idle talk about its great antiquity should be greeted with suspicion.

Newfoundland's first elected Assembly met in 1833. By 1855 it had responsible government; i.e., in effect, self-government, which it retained until 1934. But the ties to Britain were still strong. In 1869 a general election was fought on the issue of whether or not to join Canada. Confederation lost.

> Hurrah for our own native Isle, Newfoundland,
> Not a stranger shall hold one inch of its strand,
> Her face turns to Britain, her back to the Gulf,
> Come near at your peril Canadian Wolf,

a song of the time went. In 1933 Britain, in an extraordinary action unauthorized by the Newfoundland electorate, decided to suspend the financially strapped colony's constitution and, with it, elective government. Between 1934 and 1949 Newfoundland was ruled by a British-appointed commission, consisting of the governor, who was

British of course, and six commissioners (three Brits, three safe locals). This was colonialism with avengeance. On July 22, 1948, the people decided in the second of two referenda (by a vote of 78,000 to 71,000) to make Newfoundland a province of Canada, though not without considerable anguish. And some more singing, for instance this, by J.W. McGrath, called "The hero of '48" (the tune is "A mother's love is a blessing"; the politician named was the leader of the confederate party):

> A fisher boy was leaving,
> His home in Labrador,
> Fishing the same old trapskiff
> His father fished before;
> And as he was leaving his mother,
> While standing on the quay,
> He threw his arms around her neck,
> And this to her did say.

> (chorus) Don't vote confederation,
> Now that's my prayer to you,
> We own the house we live in,
> Likewise our schooner too;
> But if you vote Joe Smallwood,
> And his line of French patois,
> You'll be always paying taxes
> To the man in Ottawa.

More follows, of course. I might say that truer words than those found in the last four lines have never been spoken.

Behind the scenes in 1947-8 the British pushed Newfoundland towards confederation, which act was consummated on March 31, 1949.

The referendum of July, 1948, was a big event. Looking back on it now, we can see it somewhat in perspective. What it came down to was this: Newfoundland decided against taking the *beau risque* of independent nationhood—or of setting out on a road leading to such independence—in favor of becoming a second-class province of another country. Thus it relinquished the international dimension to life which it had enjoyed, or at any rate possessed, before 1948 and could have had, more abundantly, thereafter. This was a lot to give up. We could have become a small North Atlantic nation, out from under Britain's yoke. We could have had a seat at the U.N. and other international bodies; taken part in international conferences and sporting events; had our own embassies; owned the fish and oil off our coasts; used tariffs and exchange controls to protect local industry ... This could be extended. We would now see ourselves differently, had we taken that route. Public discourse would be on different themes. Other nations' inner turmoils would not be a big issue with us. We would have more control over our own destiny.

We traded all that for the security, such as it was, of becoming a part of Canada, inheriting, not just the benefits, but the many problems of that troubled federation. In 1949 we were hardly aware of the problems; now we are very conscious of them, especially since the province shares a border with Quebec which Quebec has never properly acknowledged. (Newfoundland won its sizable chunk of Labrador from Canada in 1927, after a prolonged battle before the British Privy Council.)

On the whole, the connection with Canada has been a mixed blessing. True, the immediate economic benefits were considerable, but had Newfoundland chosen a different path in 1948 there would still have been improvements in the quality of life here—maybe not as many as the link with Canada brought in the short term, but who knows where an independent Newfoundland might now be? In the meantime, we lost the sealing industry in the 1970s partly because of the spinelessness of the Department of External Affairs and other federal agencies, who lacked the will to defend Newfoundland's interests against international protesters. This was a blow: sealing had always played a large role in the mystique of Newfoundland, not to mention the economy. Nowadays the harp seals proliferate, causing disease in cod, damaging nets, and further depleting already devastated fish stocks. You can even see them perched on rocks near some northern communities, as if enjoying their immunity from the hunt. Also, the federal Department of Fisheries and Oceans has proven sadly to be an incompetent manager of the precious fish stocks off our coasts. These are now in such a state that on January 31, 1994, in a historic decision, the federal Minister of Fisheries and Oceans forbad even the jigging of codfish for food—thereby taking away a traditional right of Newfoundlanders, whether licensed fishermen or not. This will impact directly on tourists. Up to 1994, anyone could jig a fish in Newfoundland waters; now, nobody can.

Canada is a mentally landlocked country which has never fully understood the potential of its maritime regions. Yet the decision of 1948 inevitably meant that a flood of pushy mainland bureaucrats, academics, and other professionals would in time descend on us to influence, if not shape, the direction of the local society and economy.

It must be remembered by mainland Canadians that Newfoundland brought much into the federation in 1949: a. the greatest fishery in the world, which under federal management has been brought to the edge of extinction, b. underwater mineral resources on the continental shelf, ownership of which was given to Ottawa by the Supreme Court of Canada in 1984 following a hotly contested court case, c. the hydroelectric power and rich iron ore deposits of Labrador, both of which have contributed enormously to the economic well-being of Quebec, and d. a people filled with optimism and faith. Optimism and faith are in short supply nowadays. But the seeds of a new nationalist feeling may be taking root.

At different places in the island, you will see vestiges of our former life as a quasi-independent country. Thus the war memorial on Duckworth Street in St. John's is called the "National War Memorial." It was unveiled by British Field-Marshall Earl Haig on July 1, 1924, the eighth anniversary of the opening day of the Battle of the Somme, on which the Royal Newfoundland Regiment suffered terrible losses. July 1, Canada Day across the nation, is still termed July Drive in Newfoundland. In Notre Dame Cathedral in Paris, there is a pillar plaque which commemorates Newfoundland's contribution to the freeing of France from the German occupation. Nowadays, alas, the French, influenced more by Brigitte Bardot and other animal-rights activists than by the memory of past sacrifices made on their behalf, are likely to refer to Newfoundlanders as "tueurs de phoques," i.e., killers of seals. It was not always thus.

But to return to the visitor looking around for evidences of what Newfoundland was. You will perhaps visit the Colonial Building in St. John's, the seat of the Newfoundland legislature from 1850 to 1934, and again in 1949-59. You can hardly help but see traces of the Newfoundland Railway, now torn up, which was built in the 1880s and '90s, and which, in the Terms of Union between Newfoundland and Canada, the latter country promised to maintain. Thus, all along the TCH you will drive on "the Arnold's Cove Overpass" and other overpasses, and will wonder why the highway rises to pass over what appear to be small woods roads. Those are what is left of the railroad bed.

Numismatists among you will know that Newfoundland once had its own coins; philatelists, that we had our own stamps. We had our own passports too. There is an "Ode to Newfoundland"; the words were written by a governor, Cavendish Boyle, in the early years of this century, and remain much loved and often sung. (If you want to listen to it, you can tune in to CBC anywhere on the island; broadcasting commences each day with "O Canada" and the "Ode".) There are monuments here and there—not many—to the political heroes of earlier times, explorers, clerics, even writers. Newfoundland is unlike other Canadian provinces in that its people retain a living memory of separate nationhood. The Quebeckers say "Je me souviens," but they do not remember being a nation. We remember.

People

The word Newfoundlander is applied to anyone born in Newfoundland, though it may be stretched to include children of Newfoundlanders who were born during temporary residences overseas or on the mainland. The *Dictionary of Newfoundland English*, a scholarly work published in 1982, extends the term to embrace permanent residents as well as natives, but this is a doubtful meaning. A Scot who takes a job requiring permanent residence in St. John's is no more entitled to be called a Newfoundlander than a Newfoundlander would be to be called a Scot if he found himself in similar circumstances in Edinburgh. People born in Labrador tend to call themselves Labradorians nowadays, though they too are entitled to be called Newfoundlanders. The ancestors of Newfoundlanders were, of course, mostly Europeans.

The English dominated local history and society; even today, a large number of Englishmen and -women occupy top jobs in Newfoundland. The annual Lieutenant-Governor's garden party in St. John's resembles the one that takes place in a genteel English mansion in Katherine Mansfield's short story, and there is a highly vocal branch of the Monarchist League which takes umbrage at any imagined slight to the royal family. The Union Jack is still flown on public buildings (some private homes display them too); "God Save the Queen" is occasionally played and sung. English people who "come out" to Newfoundland find it to their advantage to retain their accents—indeed, have been known to make them more pronounced—while some local Anglophiles in St. John's east pick up useful, vaguely English accents without ever venturing across the Atlantic. But let it be said that among the English who immigrated or resided temporarily in Newfoundland, many have made significant contributions; it would be ungracious not to acknowledge them. They were, of course, the elite of the place: governors, judges, administrators, missionaries, merchants, and doctors. But I think of writers too, especially journalist Henry Winton of Exmouth, editor of a St. John's newspaper called the *Public Ledger*, a man of bulldog courage who lived to regret his ridicule of the Irish. He was caught by ruffians while riding horseback down Saddle Hill between Carbonear and Harbour Grace, Conception Bay, on May 19, 1835, was thrown to the ground, had one ear cut off and two large pieces cut out of the other, thereby becoming the butt of a famous ballad, which ended thus:

> Don't treat the poor Papists with scorn and with jeers,
> Just remember what happened to Winton's two ears!

The French had a colony at Placentia (Plaisance) until 1713, and retained the right to land and dry fish along a large portion of the coast (the so-called "French Shore") until 1904. The tiny islands of St. Pierre and Miquelon off the southern tip of the Burin Peninsula, which Newfoundland ought to have annexed early in this century, are a département of France. In a recent international tribunal, France gained ownership of a huge portion of the continental shelf adjacent to the islands, a claim which it occasionally enforces by moving one of its cruisers into the zone, armed no doubt with Exocet missiles. St. Pierre and Miquelon are a bizarre remnant of European colonialism in North America.

On the Port au Port peninsula, you will find Francophone Newfoundlanders.

The Scottish influence in Newfoundland has been strong, despite the small number of settlers. Scots have played big roles in the mercantile and professional classes in St. John's, and in agriculture in the Codroy Valley and St. George's Bay to the west. One Scot, William Carson, a doctor who came to St. John's in 1808 and died there in 1843, was a leader in the struggle for a local legislature. An important figure in medical and political history, he was also a bit of a fraud. He claimed, on landing in the New World, that he had an M.D. from Edinburgh University and stuck the letters after his name until his death; he did not in fact have the degree. However, he fought so hard for local autonomy that I, for one, am inclined to forgive him his deception. He may have been the first, but certainly wasn't the last, to acquire a degree or two in the process of crossing the North Atlantic to Newfoundland. A big gulf ferry named after him sank under mysterious circumstances in 1977. There is a humble wall plaque commemorating Carson at the foot of Cathedral Street in St. John's.

The Irish, too, were players in Newfoundland history, though by no means as influential as their numbers warranted. By the mid-1830s, 50% of the people here were Irish or of Irish descent. That percentage would drop in the decades ahead, but you will find as you drive about that the Irish brogue, Irish-looking faces, and Irish names are everywhere. At times you may even understand the complaint of visitor Philip Henry Gosse in the 19th century, who said, "I see little in [Newfoundland] but dogs and Irishmen." Listen for the Irish accent especially on the Southern Shore (the coast south of St. John's) in places such as Calvert, Ferryland, and Renews. St. Patrick's Day is a provincial government holiday in Newfoundland, and Ireland's tri-colour is sometimes displayed. (Regrettably, there is no green on the official Newfoundland flag that was adopted in 1980: an omission so glaring and pointed that I would be much disposed to think it a deliberate oversight, except that I know the flag was designed by our finest artist, Christopher Pratt, who is above such sectarian feeling. That doesn't make it any easier for me to accept, especially when I see that green is such a prominent color in Pratt's art. The pink, white, and green flag, said by some to be the unofficial flag of the people of Newfoundland, is 19th-century in origin; the colors are those of England, Scotland, and Ireland. It may be purchased, for $32 plus tax, at I.M.P. Group Ltd., 5-7 Pippy Place, St. John's, A1B 3P4; phone 722-4221.)

A visible sign of Irish influence on the island is the huge Basilica of St. John the Baptist which overlooks downtown St. John's. This edifice was built by a 19th-century bishop from the County Tipperary named Michael Anthony Fleming, who seemed to want to announce his own spiritual hegemony, or that of his church, over the capital city. The corner-stone of the structure was laid in 1841. Its shadow falls on St. Andrew's Presbyterian Kirk and the Anglican Cathedral farther down the hill. In height above sea level at least, Roman Catholicism was the dominant religion in local society.

The twin-spired Basilica of St. John the Baptist overlooks St. John's.

Mass immigration to Newfoundland from Europe was effectively over by the late 1830s. The emigrating potato-famine Irish of the 1840s passed by Newfoundland, mainly because the island was then experiencing its own famine and had no help to offer others. Thus the Irish here tend to be of an older vintage than those of New York or Ontario.

By the late 19th century, it was apparent that Newfoundlanders, whatever their origin, had developed into what Richard Howley called "a special type," with "the brand of a new life and a new land already set upon them." The culture and language of Newfoundlanders have been thoroughly studied. Their songs have been collected, their words, as mentioned earlier, put into a *Dictionary*.

Since 1949, immigrants from many countries have chosen to come and live in Newfoundland. St. John's now has something of a multicultural character, although not as pronounced as other Canadian capitals. You will find a mosque out on Logy Bay Road. There is a racial mix in certain other communities. But upheavals such as those among the Halifax, N.S., black community in July 1991, are unheard of here.

Ordinary Newfoundlanders have not yet been coarsened by tourism or infected by too much urban blight of the kind endemic, say, to southern Ontario. As Margaret Duley wrote, they have "suffered long and stayed kind." Which is to say, they tend to be courteous and helpful to visitors—rather like people in rural settings in most countries. If you follow the normal courtesies, you will be given a warm welcome.

Learn to say the word Newfoundland properly. It rhymes with understand.

Avoid telling or listening to Newfie jokes, which amount to a racial slur and which are resented by most thinking Newfoundlanders. Do not use the words Newf or Newfie; you may get a trimming if you do. Books of Newfie jokes, written mostly by Newfoundlanders out for a fast buck, are on sale, in order to pander to the tastes of ignoramuses, both the home-grown and visiting types. (I am ashamed to have to say there is even a shop called "The Newfie Store" in the Corner Brook Mall, and something called "Newfie Auto Glass" in Paradise, near St. John's; a wine labelled "Newfie Duck," to be avoided for two reasons, its name and its taste, is on sale in the liquor stores.)

Do not set up camp in a meadow or grove without asking permission to do so from the owner. Do not litter, scream, get drunk in public, tear up wildflowers, damage property, or behave in an uproarious way at hotels, restaurants, garden parties, or beaches. Do not paint signs such as "Jack & Glenda, Kenora, 1992" on rock-faces near the highway. (We are glad you came, but require no lasting memorial of your visit. Also, as you will quickly see, we are well able to deface the rocks ourselves.) If you bring small children with you, keep them under control and prevent them from being a pest to others. Ditto dogs and other pets.

When you go home, don't write a letter back to the newspapers here saying what a lovely place Newfoundland is, how hospitably you were received by the villagers, what nice accents the people have, etc. Would you write a similar letter to Yonkers, N.Y., after your visit there? Please, spare us.

Don't drive your camper or RV on the TCH at speeds of 50 or 60 kmh. If you can't drive the rig faster than that, don't bring it here.

Don't talk loudly in restaurants. Newfoundlanders regard this as the mark of a lout or fool. Raucous laughter in public places is also discouraged. Remember the poet who wrote of "the loud laugh that speaks the vacant mind"? That poet is taught here in some schools.

Eating Out; Food

I have been served overpriced swill in Italy, inedible sausage and mash in England, vegetables reduced to tasteless mush in Ireland, horrible fish-bone soup in Mexico, and "steak tartare" in Spain from which my guts took a week to recuperate; in Quebec, a friend was handed calf's brains so undercooked that I fancied I was eating in an operating room instead of a restaurant. I say this to prepare you for food in Newfoundland restaurants. It is not of the best; it is, however, getting better; and it is no worse than you will find in certain other countries and provinces. Albertan and Northern Ontario restaurants are about on a par with those in Newfoundland.

The general rule is: if you come here with a cholesterol problem, you will be sent back home in a casket. All right, I'm exaggerating! But not by a lot. It is often hard to find a decent bite to eat in restaurants outside St. John's (and in many inside St. John's). Let me catalogue some of the characteristic shortcomings of Newfoundland cuisine. Food is too often deep-fried (but if you request pan-fried or poached fish, the cook will usually provide it); very little of it is fresh, not even the fish; it may be frozen, then heated up in a microwave to pass to the unwary customer in the hope that he will not get so sick that he will sue the cook; vegetables are overdone; french fries may come out of a bag; gravy covers all; salads are smothered in dressing out of bottles; no one knows anything about wine; desserts are horrid; coffee is awful; prices are high. Most of this applies in particular to roadside gas-station restaurants, which are frequently dirty and noisy to boot, but is by no means confined to them.

You can always cook for yourself. Buy fresh produce from farmers' markets or stands by the roadside, and lobster or shrimp at the wharf or fishplant—or the supermarkets or general stores—and cook it in your own way at a picnic-area or campsite. Locally-grown vegetables —potatoes, turnip, cabbage, carrots, parsnip, and so on—are available from early August at stalls, especially around Corner Brook and Deer Lake on the west coast, near Lewisporte down north, on the Bonavista Peninsula, in the vicinity of Bay Roberts on the Conception Bay Highway, and, in St. John's, at the farmers' market on Churchill Square; so are local strawberries. You will see bakeapples and blueberries hawked by the roadside in August. There is no shortage of official places for outdoor cooking in Newfoundland, and if you don't mind sitting on rocks or stumps you can eat almost anywhere.

Cooking out can be a lot of fun, though of course it has its perils as well. However, cheap, compact pot-sets with most of the necessary utensils are available, and a lot of gear can be packed into a sturdy picnic basket. Avoid plastic knives, forks, and plates. The Coleman propane stove is a great boon to the car-camper; get one, rather than rely on the (often wet) firewood supply at campsites. If stores don't have Coleman fuel canisters, you can always use the ordinary propane tubes.

A reminder: since 1992 there has been an island-wide moratorium on the commercial cod and salmon fisheries. While it was once quite normal to buy cod and salmon on wharves or from people going door to door, this is now illegal. Don't get involved in illegal transactions. You can often buy imported cod and farmed salmon in supermarkets. Fresh scallops are sometimes available in the Port au Port area; squid in Notre Dame Bay; crab from the plant at Bay de Verde, Conception Bay (or from other Quinlan crab plants); and shrimp from the plant in Port au Choix on the Great Northern Peninsula. Go into the office at the fishplants and ask what species you can buy fresh. You will be courteously received.

Lobster and fresh farmed salmon are easy to cook. Wrap scaled salmon chunks in aluminum foil (or place them in water without the foil) and boil for 20 minutes, more if the chunks are big; put live lobsters in boiling water and leave them there for about 20 minutes. Slosh butter or margarine over both. Where can you find better meals than these? Ask around; certain bays are known for one species of fish, some for others. Unless the federal Department of Fisheries and Oceans has succeeded in killing them off along with the cod, caplin will roll onto certain beaches in late June and July, sometimes even August. These are free for the taking; you need a dip-net of some sort to get them, though sometimes you can pick them up by hand. Eat only male caplin (males are larger than females and of course have no spawn). Twist the head off, pull out the guts with the head, and discard; then fry the caplin in margarine, adding a sprinkle of pepper. Delicious! (Trout must be gutted properly, slitting the belly with a sharp knife or scissors, removing the entrails and head, and cleaning off the blood along the spine; then wash in cold water before frying.)

Occasionally, despite the joys of cooking outdoors, you will want to eat in roadside restaurants. There, in addition to some of the faults already listed, you will notice that service can be very slow. This is not because the waiters and waitresses hate tourists, the way they do, say, in Italy. Far from it. But tourism is still fairly new in these parts, and people working in restaurants and hotels can be untrained. There is as well a certain attitude towards service—a sort of *Irish* attitude. Cuban, even. To sum this up: the waiter thinks you're darned lucky to get what you ordered; he doesn't think it his duty to present you with the hot food you are paying for as quickly as he can; when he has time to serve you, he will do so. Be firm with him; tell him what you want, and when. This might work. (You will find similar levels of service in many shops, motels, campgrounds, etc. You may well catch a cold or the flu in Newfoundland, but one of the hardest things to catch is the eye of a shop clerk.)

The above judgments derive from a lifetime of dyspepsia. But I don't want to be unfair; as stated, I detect a gradual improvement in the meals served outside St. John's. New places are opening up. Try them, by all means. I also have to record that the 1993 edition of Anne Hardy's *Where to Eat in Canada*, available in bookstores across the country ($14.95), lists restaurants in the following places on the island of Newfoundland outside St. John's: Calvert, Cape Onion, Corner Brook, Deer Lake,

Gander, Glovertown, Grand Falls, Margaree, Rocky Harbour, Stephenville, Trout River, and Trouty. I suggest you buy Hardy's book and read the detailed assessments she provides. She is far from infallible but in general is a good guide.

In St. John's, the Hardy book recommends nine restaurants: Casa Grande, 108 Duckworth St. (753-6108/1177), with its branch, Quintanas de la Plaza, 57 Rowan St., Churchill Square (579-7000); The Cellar, Baird's Cove, off Water St. (579-8900); The China House, Torbay Road Mall, Torbay Road (754-2892); The India Gate, 286 Duckworth St. (753-6006), where a lunch buffet at $6.99 is an excellent bargain, and dinner prices are low as well; The Magic Wok, 402 Water St. (753-6907), featuring good Chinese food at low prices; Seafood Galley, 25 Kenmount Road (753-1255), a much-praised, cheap fish restaurant; Stella's, 183 Duckworth Street (753-9625); and The Stone House, 8 Kenna's Hill (753-2380). (Only one St. John's establishment, The Cellar, rates a single star; Hardy's best restaurants get three stars). I have a few notes to add to this. It is good to see Stella's get into Hardy's book: it serves healthy food at reasonable prices (starter, main course, coffee, one bottle of house wine, for two, including taxes and tip, $70). Stella's does not put the outrageous markup on wine that is usual in St. John's restaurants. The Cabot Club in Hotel Newfoundland, Cavendish Square (726-4980), Newman's in the Radisson Plaza Hotel on New Gower St. (739-6404), and the Woodstock Colonial Restaurant on Topsail Road (722-6933), all have their adherents, though Hardy doesn't list them. Café Duckworth, 190 Duckworth St. (722-1444) is known for its breakfast and lunch menus. The Cabot Club, Newman's, The Cellar, and The Stone House are very expensive (the last time I ate at Newman's, the fanciest restaurant in St. John's, the bill for two, including a bottle of Chablis, but no desserts, came to $140, too much; at the next fanciest, The Cellar, I paid a little less, but the fresh oysters and cajun-style poached salmon were delicious and worth the cash; at The Stone House, with a lesser wine and sticking to special menus, I paid just over $100, again too much). The Woodstock Colonial Restaurant, also expensive, features Ye Olde Newfoundland recipes such as rabbit pie ($16.95) and flipper pie (seal meat; $17.95). Quintanas de la Plaza (Mexican) has a take-out service; so does The China House, which has the best Chinese food in St. John's (but if you eat in, there is a big markup on the very limited wines); The Strand, in the Avalon Mall, off Kenmount Road (753-9077), usually has a two-for-one special price on steaks; the special starts at 2:00 p.m., Monday to Friday, at noon Saturday and Sunday. Bianca's, 178 Water St. (726-9016), has good European cuisine, not too highly priced (a couple dining out, with wine, can get away at less than $100). Hotel Newfoundland has a lunchtime smorgasboard in the place called The Outport. At Rumpelstiltskin's (579-6000), in the Journey's End Hotel, Hill o' Chips, two people can eat moderately, and drink one beer each, for

$35. In the basement of Atlantic Place, Water St., you will find a big eating area called Ports of Food, served by a half dozen fast-food establishments; I like it for a quick bite. A lot of downtown working people eat lunch there. If you're lucky, you may find a window seat and be able to see what's going on in the harbor. The House of Haynes, 207 Kenmount Road (754-4937), offers a $1.99 breakfast before noon and other "Newfie Style" food.

Auntie Crae's, located on the ground floor of a new shopping plaza on Churchill Square, is perhaps the best deli in St. John's, though some like Manna's, 342 Freshwater Rd. You can buy coffee and a sandwich at either of these places. You can get salads and sandwiches for lunch (plus the best French bread in St. John's) at Mary Jane's, 377 Duckworth St., an excellent health food shop with a small eating area (there is a tiny park near it where you can sit and eat). Manna's and Auntie Crae's also have good bread. Near Auntie Crae's you will find a little restaurant called Pasta Plus, with takeout service and a good lunch menu; soup and a sandwich, $5.25. Michel's Bakery, 799 Water St., is a French-style deli with good take-out food for picnicking.

I'll mention other eateries as we journey across the island.

Tip 10% at restaurants, 15% if you've been given good service. Tips are never automatically added to the bill.

What, you ask, are some typical Newfoundland dishes? Cod tongues, in pre-moratorium days, were standard fare, and you will still find them served (cut out of cod from Nova Scotia and the Barents Sea!). Fish and brewis is a mixture of cod and soaked sea-biscuit, covered with little pieces of fried pork fat (scruncheons); cod au gratin is cod baked in a cheese sauce (pronounce the "gratin" as if it were English); fillet of fish (fish meaning codfish; fillet—say it in English—not the French filet); moose, caribou, and partridge (in season); grilled halibut; lobster; poached or grilled salmon; jig's dinner with pease pudding; partridgeberry or blueberry pie. Corned or smoked caplin, together with smoked herring (kippers), are available in supermarkets; they are not served in most restaurants. If you want to buy local jams, you might get blueberry, partridgeberry, partridgeberry & apple, and bakeapple jams at Bidgoods Supermarket (368-3125) in the Goulds, just south of St. John's on the Southern Shore highway (route 10), a shop that specializes in Newfoundland produce. Spices? Try locally-grown savoury, available in plastic bottles in the supermarkets. For some reason, Newfoundlanders are also fond of Hard Bread (sea-biscuit or hard tack) and Excursion Bread (a softer biscuit), both manufactured locally and available in the shops. "Custard cones" is what Newfoundlanders call soft ice cream.

Drinking

Local beers and ales are of fairly good quality, and can be bought in brewers' retail outlets or many corner stores, as can Canadian brands and certain American ones produced by local breweries under licence: e.g., Miller's Lite and Coors. These cost $16.50 a dozen (rebate of $1.20 on the bottles) in January, 1994, but the price goes up almost every year owing to the insatiable maw of the tax-collectors in the provincial Department of Finance. Some taverns have beer and stout on tap. You can get imported European beer (the Dutch brand Heineken, for instance, or the French beer Kronenburg, the latter available in litre cans for $4.60) or more exotic brews such as Sapporo beer (Japanese; $9.80 for a 2-litre can) and Guinness Stout at the government-owned Liquor Store or (sometimes) the privately-owned Liquor Agency Store. Liquor and wine can be purchased only at these stores. Local brands of rum (made from Caribbean stock, bottled in St. John's) are: Screech, Big Dipper, and Cabot Tower (a proof rum). Too much is made of Screech, which has only its name to recommend it. The wise rum drinker will stick with Captain Morgan, Old Sam, Bacardi, and London Dock (Old Sam and London Dock are bottled locally, as are Smuggler's Cove and Cockspur). There are also two local brands of rye whiskey, Gold Ribbon Deluxe and Kingsway. Peter Dawson and Kenloch scotches are bottled locally. All these liquors are now very expensive: around $20-$25 for a 25-ounce bottle. And as with beer, the prices go up all the time to help pay the government's enormous salary budget. The more you drink, the more politicians and bureaucrats will be paid; perhaps this thought will keep you sober during your stay with us.

Wine is also expensive: a common Beaujolais costs $12-$15. You can get a half-decent Australian white wine for about $10; generally, anything selling for less than $10 is awful and should be used only for cooking or marinating. A lot of French wines imported to Newfoundland are corky, and I find myself drifting to Australian, Italian, American, and even Chilean brands more and more. There are German and Spanish wines around too, if you happen to like those. The most famous Newfoundland wine product is Newman's Port, which is aged and bottled in St. John's; it costs $13.50. In 1993 a blueberry wine was produced at a Markland winery (near Whitbourne) under the name Rodrigues; it sold for $8.95. A dogberry wine is expected from the same source in 1994. Watch for it.

Selection of wines is poor in the outport liquor stores, but in the larger centers you will have some choice. The best place to buy wine in St. John's is the Liquor Store in the Murray Premises, Water St., which specializes in wine, but there are good selections as well in the Elizabeth Avenue,

Kenmount Road, Churchill Square (in the shopping plaza), and Mount Pearl liquor stores. Among liqueurs, one I can recommend that has a Newfoundland flavor to it (though it is made in Finland) is a cloudberry (i.e., bakeapple) liqueur called Lapponia. It sells for $11.60 a flask. You can get a 50 ml mini-bottle for $2.35. Try it. There is a Lapponia partridgeberry (called lingonberry) liqueur as well; $11.45 a flask.

We have no molasses, but bottle our own rum; no corn or rye, but we bottle our own rye whiskey; no grapes, but we have our own wine. Cloudberries we have, yet we import cloudberry liqueur. You figure it out.

Some liquor stores have extended hours, staying open until 10 p.m. You can find out which ones by phoning 754-1100 in St. John's. Liquor agency stores may remain open until 11:00 p.m. No liquor, beer, or wine is sold from retail stores of any description on Sundays. Bars and restaurants, of course, continue to dish it out on that day.

Overpriced though the products are in these stores, it is of course cheaper to use them than the bars, where a shot of rum—less than an ounce—can cost $3.50 and up; a bottle of beer, likewise. (Even a "double" may look paltry to a thirsty man or woman, though the size of the drink is often camouflaged by a mass of ice.) If you drink during "happy hour," roughly 3:00 p.m. to 6:00 p.m., you will pay less. The markups on wine in restaurants—often 100% or more—are intolerable. With the 20% taxes, tip of 10-15%, and the markup on wine, it's obvious that eating out in Newfoundland is a luxury. Bringing your own bottle of wine to restaurants is not accepted practice in Newfoundland.

You don't have to tip every time you buy a beer at a bar in Newfoundland. Every second or third time will do.

Animals: hunting and fishing

As stated earlier, Newfoundland is a big island with a small population. Much of it is wilderness. There are undoubtedly spots in it where, in the words of Judge Prowse, "the foot of the white man has never trod" (though a friend who recently thought he was in just such a spot looked down and found an empty wiener tin at his feet). And of course there are various species of wild animals. However, I always get the feeling as I walk over the barrens or drive along the TCH that we have fewer animals than other places. Perhaps they are simply more widely dispersed, because the human population is so low. In any event, spotting a live wild animal of some sort—I mean something biggish, not a mouse or squirrel!—remains, to me, an exciting experience. We have the following mammals: moose, woodland caribou, black bear, red fox (including cross fox and silver fox), lynx, muskrat, beaver, otter, Newfoundland pine marten, ermine (weasel), arctic hare, snowshoe hare, red squirrel, mink, coyote (since 1987), eastern chipmunk, meadow vole, European bank vole (on an island in Notre Dame Bay), deer mice, Norway rat, the house mouse, masked shrew, little brown bat, eastern long-eared bat, and hoary bat. The Newfoundland wolf is extinct; an attempt to introduce bison on Brunette Island, Fortune Bay, in the 1960s was unsuccessful; the Newfoundland pine marten, a unique sub-species of marten confined largely to the Little Grand Lake area, is an endangered species, now numbering less than 500 (though an effort has been made to introduce them in Terra Nova National Park); we have no badgers, skunks, porcupine, or raccoons. No reptiles. An occasional snake is found, but it is presumed that it has been brought in from Nova Scotia. Frogs are by no means as common as they are elsewhere, but we do have the green frog all over the island, and some striped coarse frog, wood frog, and northern leopard frogs; the American toad is found near Steady Brook, just east of Corner Brook. Taken all together, this does not seem a long roll call.

Do you like killing wild animals? I have to tell you that just looking at them is much more to my liking, and that bringing down a 1,000-pound moose with a bullet from a .303 rifle is a long way from being my idea of a good time. I am not a vegetarian; I have been on hunting parties in the deep woods of Newfoundland; I have seen dead moose and caribou gutted, skinned, and quartered. The pleasure all this gives eludes me; I imagine it is akin to what is felt in the slaughterhouse. Oscar Wilde defined fox-hunters as "the unspeakable in pursuit of the uneatable," and I certainly have no wish to apply the first two words to the hunters I have known. But let's face it, the word "uneatable" does apply, to some extent, to moose, woodland caribou, and black bear—the "big game" in Newfoundland. And since these animals are essentially undesirable as food, I sometimes wonder why people want to hunt them. (At the same time, I know that culling the moose population is necessary in view of the danger they present on the highways.)

Fishing? That's different—at least it is to me. I can think of few pleasures greater than fishing for salmon or trout in Newfoundland. So my advice is: bring your fishing gear, a fly-rod if you plan to chase salmon, a spinning-rod if you want to go after trout in the lakes and ponds. (You are not permitted to use spinning rods, or any line with something other than a fly-hook on it, in scheduled salmon rivers.) These are the fish species on the island: brook trout (often called mud trout), which are found all over; brown trout (mostly the Avalon); rainbow trout (the Avalon); Arctic char (Gander Lake, Western Brook Pond, and other places); salmon; and landlocked salmon (ouananiche). There are no pike, walleye, lake-trout, suckers, perch, or bass; there are eels, if you know a way to catch those. You can always buy rods, creels, etc. in Newfoundland, if you want. In Corner Brook, shop for these items at

Barnes Sporting Goods, 16 Humber Road (634-2291); in St. John's, try The Sports Shop, 256 Water St. (722-3344). And virtually anywhere on the island you can buy bamboo poles, fishing line, bobbers, hooks, spinners, and worms for bait. My point is: for a few dollars, you can go trouting in roadside ponds, and possibly get as many fish as many who use very expensive equipment. (Note: I said *possibly*.) You will be able to tell the good ponds from the number of local residents with lines out in them. Newfoundlanders fish along the TCH right across the island.

Having told you all that, I have to add that there are restrictions on fishing by non-residents in Newfoundland. Of course, non-residents cannot fish for trout or salmon without a licence, which can be purchased at shops everywhere on the island. For trout: individual licence $5, family licence (to include children 17 and under) $10; for salmon: individual licence $10, family $15. I was given these figures early in 1994; they could go up fast. (A resident may fish for trout without a licence, but requires a licence for salmon.) But here's the catch: a non-resident may not fish on a scheduled salmon river unless accompanied by a licensed guide (if, however, he is a non-resident returning Newfoundlander, he may do so if accompanied by a direct relative; see below). Also, a non-resident may not fish for trout on any "unscheduled water," i.e., pond, lake, or stream, that is beyond 800 meters from a provincial highway (defined as one with a route number on the map) unless accompanied by a guide (or, if a non-resident returning Newfoundlander, by a direct relative). Get this straight: *within* the 800-meter (roughly, half-mile) limit, you may fish for trout to your heart's content, as long as you have a licence; *beyond* it, you must have a guide.

Just to clear up the point about the non-resident returning Newfoundlander. Let's say you are one. If you have a father, mother, son, daughter, brother, sister, or in-law who is a resident, you may use him or her as a guide.

Get the picture? Simple, isn't it? (You may feel better in the woods with a measuring tape, genealogical chart, and birth certificate.)

To comfort you, let me repeat that many Newfoundlanders fish a few yards from the sides of highways. I suggest you find out what the rules are. Get these two pamphlets: *Non-Resident Anglers: Newfoundland and Labrador* from the Department of Tourism and Culture, Government of Newfoundland and Labrador, P.O. Box 8700, St. John's, A1B 4J6; and the *Angler's Guide* from: Department of Fisheries & Oceans, Box 5667, St. John's, A1C 5X1. An up-to-date *Angler's Guide* is vital, since the Department of Fisheries & Oceans has made substantial changes in bag limits and other matters pertaining to trout in 1994. There is also a quota—even zonal quotas—on salmon, and if these quotas have been met you will be restricted to a "catch-and-release" method. Many anglers find this unbearable. If your heart is set on catching and keeping a salmon or two, you would be wise to phone ahead to the federal Department of Fisheries & Oceans (709-772-5997/5482) to see if this is possible.

The restrictions regarding guides mentioned above are fairly recent. No doubt ardent anglers among you will resent the way the provincial government is forcing you to hire guides, whom you very well may not need. I share your concern, though I have to say that one reason for the tighter regulations is overfishing by tourists. The columnist Bill Power has graphically drawn attention to such abuse of privilege prior to 1990, pointing to fishing spots depleted by "non-residents camped by the hundreds, in everything from pickup trucks with refrigeration units to trailer homes with deep freezes." Another factor leading to tighter regulation is lobbying by professional guides who, like private campground operators, want a piece of the action in the tourist "business." The latter have been particularly vocal. It may not take long before they persuade the bureaucrats to outlaw what is called "gravel-pit camping"; i.e., camping just off the road, for free. This will obviously make it more expensive for people to travel here and enjoy a holiday. I note in a recent government "consultation paper" the ominous statement that "The tourism industry in Newfoundland and Labrador offers considerable potential for expansion." In time, a Newfoundland holiday will cost as much as one in Italy, where you can hardly pass your water without paying a fee to the authorities.

Speaking of water, I suggest you think seriously about bringing a canoe with you to Newfoundland (or buying one during your visit). That is, if you know how to use one; canoes in the hands of inexperienced people are very dangerous toys, and drownings from canoes are not uncommon here. I know a canoe on top of a car can be a nuisance to the traveller, but there are so many wonderful ponds and rivers in Newfoundland that you will miss a lot of fun if you don't get out on them. In my opinion, canoes should never be used on the salt water; and I wouldn't recommend using them in the big inland lakes such as Red Indian Lake and Grand Lake (see below under "Grand Lake") unless you are well trained. Grand Lake in particular can have waves as big as the ocean's. Some rivers are suitable for extended canoe trips, and you can get on them without a lot of trouble: e.g., the Gander, Northwest Gander, Indian, and Terra Nova rivers. The Main River, which flows from Four Ponds on the Great Northern Peninsula into Sop's Arm in White Bay, is a fast-water river that should be attempted only by expert canoeists. To get to the headwaters of the Main and to other remote rivers and lakes, you will have to hire a float-plane. For detailed information on canoe routes in Newfoundland, write to Parks Division, Department of Tourism and Culture (address above); phone 729-2424/6205.

To go back to what I just said: do not bring a canoe to Newfoundland, or buy one here, unless you are an experienced canoeist. *Always wear a life-jacket in a canoe.* Certain life-jackets now on the market allow virtually unrestricted movement. The Canadian Red Cross publishes a pamphlet called "Anglers and Hunters Safe Boating Guide," available free, and well worth reading.

Hunting and fishing happen to be the most highly developed and regulated aspects of Newfoundland's tourist industry. There are many professional big-game outfitters, some specializing in particular animals, and there are fishing lodges all over the island. Two pamphlets you need to get are: the provincial government's *Hunting Guide*, published annually by the Department of Tourism and Culture (address above; phone 709-576-2830/0862 or, toll-free, 1-800-563-6353), giving essential information about regulations, hunting areas, quotas, closed areas, field techniques for shooting moose, etc., and *Newfoundland & Labrador Hunting & Fishing Guide*, published annually by the same department, which provides the names and addresses of outfitters, together with other relevant information. Both are free. If all you want to do is look at animals, that's free too.

Other sports

Sports fans should know that there's little or nothing in the way of professional sports activity in Newfoundland. (But the St. John's Maple Leafs, the AHL farm team of the Toronto Maple Leafs, commenced play in fall, '91.) There is some amateur sport—baseball, softball, soccer, hockey—but it is of fairly low caliber. However, I hear the softball is good, though you can't tell this from the size of the paunches of some of those playing it, and you evidently have to be obese to be a coach or executive in the sport in St. John's. Perhaps the best baseball in Newfoundland is played in Corner Brook; the best soccer, on the Burin Peninsula. The level of rugby in St. John's has been improving dramatically in recent years, and there is now an excellent pitch—in fact, two pitches—with clubhouse, owned by the Swilers' Rugby Club off Crosbie Road (where from time to time you can buy, for $15, a pink, white, and green t-shirt with the words "Republic of Newfoundland" on it). Other rugby clubs are well organized as well (the Dogs have a neat clubhouse at 57 New Gower St.). A development team from the New Zealand All-Blacks, possibly the best rugby players in the world, passed through in 1990, and excellent Irish, English, and American teams play in St. John's from time to time.

Now golf. As elsewhere, you will pay green fees of $20 and up for 18 holes at Newfoundland golf courses. There is a public 9-hole golf course off Nagle's Hill in St. John's north. Book (753-7110) a tee time at least 24 hours ahead. The course opens at 6:00 a.m. and closes at dark. Some starter equipment may be rented, but you are expected to bring your own clubs.

Anyone living off the Avalon Peninsula can golf at the Bally Haly Golf and Country Club, Logy Bay Road, St. John's, if he or she finds a club member to play with. Phone 24 hours ahead to book a tee time (726-5400). Green fees in 1993 were $33 for 18 holes; clubs may be rented.

The Terra Nova Park Lodge in Port Blandford, A0C 2G0 (phone 543-2525) operates the 18-hole Twin Rivers Golf Course in Terra Nova National Park. If you write, the Lodge will send you a course guide with all relevant information. I stayed at this establishment for a night in July, 1991, when it was known as St. Christopher's Resort. Many wrinkles remained to be ironed out. I understand improvements have been made since then.

You can generally rent clubs at the following, but phone ahead to book a tee time or make arrangements to play: Gander Golf Club (256-4653); Grand Falls Golf Club (489-9068); Blomidon Golf Club in Corner Brook (634-5550); Harmon Golf and Country Club in Stephenville (643-4322).

Tennis courts are often available in the larger towns, and even in some smaller ones; ask locally for directions. In St. John's, Riverdale Tennis Club, Rennies Mill Road (579-6600), will let visitors from outside St. John's book a court and play (for a fee, of course); there is also a Green Belt Tennis Club on Newtown Road (722-3840), which allows non-members access to indoor and outdoor courts.

In Corner Brook and Gander, there are public swimming pools in the Arts and Culture Centres; the Aquarena, Westerland Road, St. John's (576-8164; 576-8626 for the swim schedule), is an excellent facility for swimming; the cost of entry to the pool is $2.75 for an adult, $1.75 for a child (ditto at the H.G.R. Mews Community Centre pool on Mundy Pond Road, 576-8499; swim schedule, 576-8408). If you want to swim without paying in St. John's, find your way to Three-Pond Barrens in Pippy Park, north of the city. It is not very far from the Marine Institute; locate that institution, keep going west along Ridge Road, head north on Nagles Hill Road. You will have to park your car and walk for a half mile to the first pond along a well-trodden path. Leave valuables in the locked car. Perhaps you should have changed into your swim-suit in the car, but you can always do it in the trees. This is a common occurrence near the pond; no one notices or cares. And if someone does notice, what odds? See that wharf? Dive off it. The pond—indeed, Pippy Park generally—is one of the chief attractions of St. John's. Government officials, who a few years back wanted to put a highway through a tunnel under St. John's, now intend to build an arterial road through Pippy Park. This is part of the enduring fantasy in the heads of the city fathers and mothers: the fantasy that St. John's is an industrial city. As you can readily see, there is *no* industry in St. John's.

In smaller communities, ask where the best swimming hole is, or simply where the closest deep pond is. You are never far from fresh water in Newfoundland.

For information on yachting, write the Royal Newfoundland Yacht Club, P.O. Box 869, Manuels, Conception Bay, A1W 1N4 (834-8622). A book by Rob Mills, *Coastal Cruising: Newfoundland*, is available in local bookstores for $18.95.

Annual rowing regattas are held in St. John's (first Wednesday in August), Harbour Grace (last weekend in July), Placentia (around mid-July), Lower Island Cove, Conception Bay (mid- to late August), and other towns. These normally are civic holidays, and are accompanied by much festivity.

Cycling. You can rent good mountain bikes and equipment (together with a roof rack for your car) from Earle Industries, 51 Old Pennywell Road, St. John's (576-1951). Rates in 1994: $25 per day, $119 per week. The owner, Harold Earle, is a cycling and kayaking enthusiast. What with rainy weather, wind, hills, and (usually) unpaved shoulders on highways, cycling is hard in Newfoundland. Cyclists nonetheless are seen often on the TCH and elsewhere, gamely toiling on. If it's your game, go for it. *The Best Bicycle Tours of Eastern Canada*, by Jerry Dennis ($20), includes tours of the Avalon Peninsula and Gros Morne (and vicinity).

Skiing. See "Corner Brook and vicinity," below, for Marble Mountain. Barnes Sporting Goods in Corner Brook is a store that specializes in ski equipment. While you're out west, you might try cross country skiing at Gros Morne National Park; write for the pamphlet "Cross Country Skiing" (see "Gros Morne," below, for address). The White Hills resort near Clarenville (466-7773) is well regarded by some skiers.

Scuba-diving. Get your hands on *Newfoundland and St. Pierre*, by David N. Barron, which is the first volume of the Atlantic Diver Guide ($14.95).

Ocean-kayaking is becoming a popular sport in the province. Obviously, it is of benefit to those who want to get close to bird colonies or whales. Obviously, too, it requires training and practice before it may be considered safe. You must wear a wet suit when engaged in this activity. Contact Eastern Edge Outfitters (Jim or Margie Price at 782-1465) to book kayaking tours to Random Island and elsewhere; write for prices and information to the company at Box 17, Site 14, R.R. # 2, Paradise, Nfld., A1L 1C2.

Arts and crafts

To turn to the subject of the arts and crafts in Newfoundland. First, the performing arts. Summer is a good time to attend folk festivals, which take place in many parts of the island in July and August, are held outdoors (except when it rains), and are a lot of fun. You will hear chin-music, spoon-players, fiddlers, folk bands, accordionists, singers, reciters, etc.; and see displays of crafts, step-dancers, and other performers. (See "Gifts to take back with you," at the end of this book, where I recommend good tapes and CDs.) You will also be able to buy local soul-food like gandies and toutens, and beer. Newfoundland ranks high among Canadian provinces in per-capita consumption of beer, but I have never run into rowdiness at folk festivals. This doesn't mean there isn't any, just that I haven't seen it. There is a comradeship at such festivals that is infectious. They are cheap to get into, perhaps $5. They are, in my experience, far more enjoyable than the parish "garden-parties," which are held on Sundays in summer to support various churches and consist mostly of low-level gambling and childish games, or even the regattas held in some of the bigger towns. (See "Other sports," above.) When you arrive on the island, get your hands on an annual publication called *Newfoundland and Labrador Folk Festival Guide*, which is widely distributed and tells you what's going on, and when. The biggest festivals tend to be: the Newfoundland and Labrador Folk Festival, St. John's, early August; the Hangashore Festival, Corner Brook, mid-July; the Exploits Valley Salmon Festival, Grand Falls-Windsor, third weekend in July; the Brimstone Head Festival, Fogo, mid-July; and the Conception Bay Folk Festival, Carbonear, late July. Get the exact dates before setting out for these places.

I'm afraid that the Stephenville Festival (see below, "Stephenville and Port au Port") and the folk festivals are about the only performing arts you will find on the island in summer, outside St. John's. Certain communities (Corner Brook, Gander, Grand Falls, and St. John's) have what are termed Arts and Culture Centres, which are in fact government-run theatres, but no one in the provincial cabinet has any interest in the arts and these white elephants are largely inactive in summer (indeed, some are inactive most of the year) and exist mostly to provide managers and security staff with salaries; this is true even of the one in the capital city, which cost taxpayers an enormous sum to build. (The pools in the Corner Brook and Gander centres, however, give them some usefulness.) There *is* professional theatre in St. John's in summer, at the LSPU Hall, Victoria St. (753-4531); it tends to be avant-garde. Watch for the following names: Andy Jones, Cathy Jones, Greg Malone, Mary Walsh, Bernie Stapleton, Amy House, Michael

Chaisson, Rick Boland, and Rick Mercer. These are the best professional actors in Newfoundland. If you get a chance to see Andy Jones, Cathy Jones, or Mary Walsh, go. They are superb performers.

Among the best local singers are: Ron Hynes, Pamela Morgan, Anita Best, Shirley Montague, Dave Panting, Mary Barry, and Phyllis Morrissey. The finest performing group (consisting of Kevin Blackmore, Raymond Johnson, and Wayne Chaulk) is termed Buddy Wassisname and the Other Fellers. They cod around a lot on stage as well as sing, but are exceptionally talented. Fight to get in to hear them. The Irish Descendants, Colcannon, and Great Big Sea are other groups well worth hearing. Accordionists? Art Stoyles, Frank Maher, and Minnie White. Jazz? Watch for saxophonist John Nugent, who sometimes comes to town and plays. The Duke of Duckworth, a pub at 325 Duckworth St., St. John's (actually in an alley off the street) has live music from time to time, usually jazz. The Ship Inn, 265 Duckworth St. (in another alley), sometimes has music on Saturday nights, and every Tuesday at 9:30 p.m. (cover around $2) it features local entertainers ("Wom/men Jammin'"). This is a pub where artists hang out; good atmosphere; good beer.

You can buy tapes and CDs of local groups in many shops; but I recommend Fred's, 198 Duckworth St., and O'Brien's Music Store, 278 Water St., St. John's.

Every second summer in St. John's, on even years, a "Sound Symposium" takes place over a two-week period in July. There are concerts, plays, exhibitions of various types, and a "harbor symphony"—ships' whistles, foghorns, etc.— associated with this activity. There aren't many ships using the harbour these days; the "symphony" isn't loud.

From 1994 to '97, you may run into "historical" pageants in different communities, put on with money provided by the federal government to help "develop tourism." Be prepared for much talk of the oldest this and the oldest that, "authentic" costumes, pirates walking the plank, greedy merchants, captured Beothucks, exploited settlers, and so on.

To turn to the visual arts. Many fine painters and printmakers have worked or are working on the island, and there are Newfoundlanders living on the mainland who sell their work in the galleries here. The best known of all these are undoubtedly Christopher Pratt and Mary Pratt, but I suggest that the following are also artists of high quality: David Blackwood, Conrad Furey, Reginald Shepherd, Helen Parsons Shepherd, Scott Goudie, Donna Clouston (who does lovely silkscreens), Janice Udell, Derek Caines, Sylvia Bendzsa, Peter Bell, Paul Parsons, Pam Hall, I. Hoenig, Kate Graham, Gerald Squires, Tish Holland, Ann Meredith Barry, Di Dabinett, Jon Wilkinson, and Sid Butt. Nor are these all who count. I like Katherine Munro's miniature watercolors of St. John's and the outports, which are inexpensive.

Photographers are at work in Newfoundland as well; there are books of photographs in the bookstores and gift shops. The photographer Don Lane has a gallery in Hotel Newfoundland in St. John's.

Now, art galleries. There is a public gallery, operated by Memorial University, in the St. John's Arts and Culture Centre (737-8209). It has a permanent collection—the finest collection of Newfoundland art in the world. The gallery stays open in summer and is a must-see for anyone with an interest in the visual arts. (It will take time to find your way to it. The Arts and Culture Centre was constructed in the 1960s, when architects liked to pretend that buildings didn't have doors. So they hid doorways.) There are, from time to time, art exhibitions in the Arts and Culture Centres elsewhere on the island—that is, if they are open for business—featuring artists from the local region, and you may be able to pick up excellent pieces at low to moderate prices. Should the Centre be closed down, you may find that artists are exhibiting and selling elsewhere; thus when the Arts and Culture Centre in Corner Brook effectively shut its doors in summer, 1991, local artists opened a gallery in the Corner Brook Mall, where you could buy good work for between $100 and $500. This is a low range of prices. Please remember: artists are professional people, and if you want to take a painting or print back with you, be prepared to pay a good price for it. The following are private galleries: The Ewing Gallery, in the Glynmill Inn, Corner Brook (634-4577); Greg Seaward Gallery, 111B Memorial Drive, Gander (651-3101); Topsail Art Gallery, 13 Woodpath Road, Chamberlains, Conception Bay (834-3612); and in St. John's, Emma Butler Gallery, 111 George St. (739-7111), Christina Parker Fine Art, 7 Plank Road (753-0580), Spurrell Gallery, 87 Long's Hill (753-6600), James Baird Gallery, 221 Duckworth St. (726-4723), A.M. Carew Art Gallery, 168 Water St. (726-6869; photos, paintings, and sculpture), and Wild Things, 124 Water St. (722-3335; nature art and photography, adventure tours, etc.). Eastern Edge Gallery, Baird's Cove, off Water St. (739-1882), is an artist-run space, as is the gallery in the basement of the LSPU Hall (see above); both open in the afternoons, Tuesday through Saturday.

Some institutions have artwork of significance. The Presentation Convent, a building attached to the east side of the Roman Catholic Basilica, St. John's, has a sculpture called "The Veiled Virgin," by Giovanni Strazza, which was brought to Newfoundland in 1862. It is definitely worth seeing, and if you call at the convent you will be shown it without an appointment. Under the high altar in the Basilica is "The Redeemer in Death" by the Irish sculptor John Hogan, done in 1850, a fine work. Atlantic Place, Water St., St. John's, has a big mural by Reginald Shepherd on the first floor. Gerald Squires painted the Last Supper and the Stations of the Cross for Mary, Queen of the World parish church on Topsail Road, near St. John's. You will find sculptures in the vicinity of Confederation Building, the seat of the provincial government that overlooks St. John's. I withhold judgment on these.

Books. Newfoundland now has a number of very good writers, and there have been, since the seventeenth century, authors like Farley Mowat, Claire Mowat, Franklin Russell, and David Macfarlane who have come in from the outside to "discover" the place anew and write books about it. Russell and Macfarlane are fine writers, and I wouldn't wish to slight them. But try the good local writers. See "Gifts to take back with you," towards the back of this *Guide*, where I recommend what I think are the books visitors are most likely to be interested in. St. John's bookstores? Dicks and Co., Scotia Centre, Water St. (579-3308); Word Play, 221 Duckworth St. (726-9193); Coles bookshop in the Avalon Mall (753-3394); Smith Books, Avalon Mall (754-0791); Readmore in the Village Mall (364-2073); Bennington Gate, Terrace in the Square, Churchill Park (576-6600). For children's books, try Granny Bates, 2 Bates Hill (739-9233). Breakwater Books retails its own titles, 100 Water St. (722-6680).

Afterwords Book Store, 166 Water St., St. John's (753-4690), has copies of historic photos, including the celebrated shot of the iceberg-Madonna gliding past the Narrows.

To crafts. There are numerous craftsmen and -women working in Newfoundland. Two big craft fairs are held annually in the St. John's Memorial Stadium (early July; and late November-early December), and one in Corner Brook at the Glynmill Inn (late November). So there are crafts on sale everywhere, but especially the west coast and the Avalon. For a free *Official Guide to the Craft Shops and Studios of Newfoundland and Labrador*, a valuable community-by-community guide to craft shops, hobby shops, and the like, updated annually, write Craft Development Division, Department of Tourism and Culture, 136 Crosbie Road, St. John's, A1B 3K3 (or phone 729-7182). For other information, contact The Newfoundland and Labrador Crafts Development Association, P.O. Box 5295, St. John's, A1C 5W1 (phone 753-2749).

Some exquisitely crafted items come out of Newfoundland and are marketed nationally. Watch especially for: sealskin products and Grenfell parkas in northern Newfoundland, especially around St. Anthony (also in St. John's); Winterhouses knitted goods, especially attractive sweaters, available at Newfoundland Weavery, 177 Water St., St. John's; Nonia knitwear and woven placemats (sold at the Nonia shop at 286 Water St., St. John's); products by Bogside Weaving (209 New Gower St., St. John's), which are sold in the company's own shop, and at Nonia, the Newfoundland Weavery, and (some items) The Salt Box, 194 Duckworth St., St. John's; Yarn Point Crafts knitwear in Mose Ambrose and elsewhere; and hooked mats in Placentia Bay, around Conception Bay, and on the Southern Shore. (I especially recommend Nonia, Winterhouses, and Bogside products. Generally, scarves, mitts, and sweaters are good gifts to take back.) Melendy's, 336 Water St., St. John's (753-8021) has a wide variety of souvenirs and crafts, as does Laracy's, 324 Water St. (753-7775). Some vulgar items, e.g., "Newfie" mugs with the handle inside, are on sale in certain shops. Choose quality. Handcrafted goods are not subject to the provincial retail sales tax. Devon House Craft Centre at 59 Duckworth St., St. John's (753-2749), is a combination gallery and gallery shop, featuring mainly Newfoundland and Labrador crafts.

For a good selection of sweatshirts and t-shirts with Newfoundland themes, try Island Beach Co., 301 Water St., St. John's (579-3655).

Getting your taxes back

Newfoundlanders are taxed to death, but that's no reason why you should be. As a tourist from out of the province, you are eligible to get rebates on Retail Sales Tax (RST); keep your receipts, and when you get home write for a "Tourist Rebate Form" to Department of Finance, Tax Administration Branch, Box 8720, St. John's, A1B 4K1. If you come from out of the country, you are also entitled to a federal Goods and Services Tax (GST) rebate: again, keep your receipts, and when you get home write for a "GST Rebate for Visitors" form to Revenue Canada, District Excise Office, P.O. Box 5500, St. John's, A1C 5W4. Do send for these forms, and return them. You will get some money back, and you will keep the wheels of "industry" humming in Newfoundland. Write to the offices before coming to find out which receipts you should keep. The general rule is: you cannot claim rebates on food, gasoline, and other items consumed here, but you may make claims on gifts, clothing, etc. taken out of the province or country. A partial GST rebate (but not RST) may be obtained for hotel and motel charges.

Starting off from Port aux Basques; Driving on the TCH; Where to Stay; Birds; Berries; Codroy Valley

As a general rule, I would not come to Newfoundland expecting to use public transportation. But there *is* public transportation on the island. The CN Roadcruiser Service operates between St. John's and Port aux Basques (737-5912; $79.75 one way, double that for the return trip). In addition, there are private bus companies, mini-vans, and outport taxis.

Thus the Viking Express (634-4710) goes from Corner Brook to St. Anthony ($41 one way); Guy Bailey's Bus Service (532-4642) links Corner Brook and Baie Verte ($23); Newhook's Transportation Ltd. (726-4876; 227-5597) runs from the Marine Atlantic ferry terminal in Argentia, Placentia Bay, to St. John's ($10); Devin's bus line (886-2955/2576; 634-7777) operates between Corner Brook-Stephenville and Burgeo (Corner Brook to Burgeo, $28); the Bay D'Espoir Bus Service (538-3429) connects St. Alban's and Grand Falls ($25); the Fleetline buses (722-2608; 229-7600) ply between St. John's and Carbonear ($8); the Bonavista North Transportation Ltd. (579-3188) sends a bus from St. John's to Musgrave Harbour in Bonavista Bay ($40); other buses (Squires'; 722-5218) go from St. John's along the north side of Conception Bay to Sibley's Cove in Trinity Bay (and along the entire eastern shore of Trinity Bay); Cheeseman's and Slaney's mini-vans go down the Burin Peninsula from St. John's; and so on. The best way to get information about these buses is through local sources; but, within reason, you can fairly well count on there being ground transportation between various districts and towns. (Prices quoted as of January, 1994.) Buses we have. But thanks to the duplicity of federal politicians, and to the timidity of local ones, there are no trains; and unless you are young and full of beans, you wouldn't want to spend too much time in buses and outharbor taxis. You either have to drive (and ferry) here or fly in and rent a car. The latter is obviously the more expensive option, though many reasons can be found for preferring it. Hertz and other big rental companies operate in Newfoundland. In 1994 I was quoted the following price by Hertz for a new Chrysler Voyager van, holding 7 people: $52.95 per day, with 100 km free, 20 cents for each extra km; or $305 per week, with 700 free km, again 20 cents for each extra km. Plus taxes of course. Add gasoline too: about 60 cents per litre. It seems to me to make more sense to rent a vehicle if you are coming from far away: Edmonton, say, or Las Vegas. As I said earlier, there's not much point in coming to Newfoundland for a two-week vacation and sticking in one spot. Move around; see the sights.

What kind of vehicle are you bringing with you? If you have something called Old Nellie that you have driven for about 200,000 km, leave it home. Do not inflict your wreckage on the people of Newfoundland! The highways here are being upgraded, but there are still quite a number of dirt roads off the main routes and some of the paved ones are rough in spots. It's a big, empty island: far bigger than Ireland. A breakdown is a serious matter. So bring a good vehicle, with new or hardly used tires. Maybe you should join the Canadian Automobile Association before coming; it reimburses you for towing charges, and offers other advantages. (There is no Newfoundland branch, but Nova Scotia has one. Write: CAA Maritimes Ltd., P.O. Box 9500, Stn. A, Halifax, Nova Scotia B3K 5P8; phone 902-443-5530). You will probably get a flat tire during your stay here. Do you know how to change a tire? If you don't, learn how to do so. Can you loosen the lugs on every wheel? Try each lug in turn and make sure you can remove them if you have too. These have to be on tight, of course, but they are now put on with such force by incompetent mechanics at garages that the bolts often break off when you try to unscrew them. I have met tourists by the side of the road with two or three broken bolts in their hands. Putting some hard grease on each bolt early in the life of your car can help in the event that you have to take the lug off. One further hint: the long jack-handle wrench that comes with many cars, if applied with force to lugs, has the effect of buckling and weakening the bolt. Far better to use a star wrench, which can be obtained from a Canadian Tire store for about $10. Make sure you get one that fits your lugs. (If the long wrench also serves as a jack-handle, don't throw it away!)

But let's say you buy a new car, drive to North Sydney, N.S., overcome the Byzantine routines of Marine Atlantic, and board the ferry for Port aux Basques—once a prosperous railway terminal, now a community whose economy is somewhat precarious.

Welcome to the island.

You have come in July or August? That's when everyone comes. In September or even October the weather can still be half-decent—no promises!—and there is far less tourist traffic. One difficulty in coming in the fall is that the provincial government closes down most of its parks after Labor Day weekend, thereby limiting opportunities to camp. (But Butterpot, Notre Dame, Barachois, Cheesman, Dildo Run, Lockston Path, Fitzgerald's Pond, and Pistolet Bay parks stayed open until Thanksgiving—i.e., October 11—in 1993.) Since camping out is possible in early fall, or even later, and a lot of people use RVs in any case, I've never been sure that closing parks so early made a lot of sense. Certain campgrounds in the two national parks stay open until Thanksgiving, and there is even limited winter camping in them. Autumn colors in Newfoundland, where there are plenty of deciduous trees among the evergreens, are spectacular.

Ok, so you've chosen summer. The first thing you will need is a map. The most readily available one is the freely distributed "Official Highway Map," published by the Department of Tourism and Culture, Government of Newfoundland and Labrador. You will have no trouble getting your hands on this, but if you want to have one prior to coming, write to the office (the address is given on page 29). There are many defects in this map, but it'll do. You'll find a "Vinlander Tourist Map" of Newfoundland, and other maps, on sale in the shops, but the free one is better. If you are including Newfoundland within an Atlantic Canadian vacation, you might do well to buy "Atlantic Canada: Vacation Guide Map," from MapArt Corporation, 72 Bloor St. E., Oshawa, Ontario L1H 3M2. This is listed at $2.95, though it will cost you more in certain outlets. Detailed topographic maps of the island are available. These maps (scale: 1:50,000) may be obtained from Department of Environment and Lands, Air Photo Map Library, Howley Building, Higgins Line, St. John's, A1B 4J6 (phone 729-3305), for $9.82 (if purchased in the province) or $8.77 (if ordered from outside the province, plus a shipping charge of $5.35; $3.20 extra for COD). Name the precise area for which you want the topographic map, and one will be sent to you. You will need maps of this nature if you are planning wilderness travel.

The second thing you must have is the provincial government publication entitled *Newfoundland and Labrador Travel Guide*, a new edition of which is published each year. This is full of official bluster and nonsense about scenery, history, the great outdoors, heritage, etc., and as you will quickly see when you try to use it, it is poorly laid out. But it lists events, licenced accommodations, federal, provincial, and municipal parks, crafts stores, possible auto routes, plus much more. And of course it too is free. You can get one at the Visitor Information Centre at the ferry terminal in North Sydney, or at the Provincial Interpretation Centre in Port aux Basques. (Provincial-government information centers, highly useful institutions, are located at various places on the island; some towns have municipal centers as well.) If you want to have a *Travel Guide* before coming, write to the Department of Tourism, address on page 29. Let me repeat the toll-free number, 1-800-563-6353.

There is also a *Newfoundland and Labrador Vacation Guide*, published annually by the CFCB Radio Network, and distributed free. It is available at Holiday Inns and other places on the island, but you can get a copy by writing: CFCB, P.O. Box 570, Corner Brook, A2H 6H5 or dropping by the station at 345 O'Connell Drive (phone: 634-4570). This has maps, routes, ads, helpful hints, and much more. I recommend you get a copy.

I presume you have decided where to stay during your visit to Newfoundland. My preferred method is camping, and I have a light, expensive tent which can be erected in about ten minutes, packs neatly into a small carrier bag, and accommodates two people. (My sleeping bags also squeeze into small shapes.) There are campsites all over the island: again, if I can state my own preference, I like to camp in the two national parks (Gros Morne and Terra Nova) or the various provincial parks (74 in number, but only 41 allow camping). Your *Travel Guide* (see two paragraphs above) and map will tell you where the provincial parks are, and whether you can camp in them. The signposts on the roads will give you the same information. The parks have well-placed sites, plus garbage cans, fireplaces, firewood, picnic tables, rudimentary toilets, and a supply of drinking water from taps. So do Gros Morne and Terra Nova. Only one provincial park, Grand Codroy, in the southwest corner of the island, has full services (i.e., water, sewer, and electricity) for trailers; not even our national parks have these. Grand Codroy, Barachois, Blow Me Down, Pistolet Bay, and Dildo Run provincial parks have flush toilets and showers. Camping fees at provincial parks are $7 per night; the national parks charge more. (In 1993 there was no vehicle entry fee at provincial parks, so you had free access to picnic sites and beaches; national parks make you buy a vehicle licence.) There are also municipal parks in certain localities, and private campgrounds.

Provincial parks are normally great places to camp or set up your RV, but they can vary in quality, depending on certain factors: how diligent the attendants are, how often the toilets (crude outhouses really, and they can be very offputting) are treated with chemicals to reduce odor, how close the camping area is to the highway, how much use is made of the park by local residents, how the previous tenant has treated your particular site, etc. On long weekends the parks are sometimes frequented by drunks, partypeople, and fans of AM rock-radio. Not all the smoke wafting towards you is woodsmoke; not all the music, Beethoven. Some parks in the vicinity of St. John's are notorious for displays of assorted brands of vulgarity. I would think twice about spending a summer weekend in them. If you are unlucky enough to find yourself camped next to a crowd of drunks, you may have to complain loudly and often to the park attendants to get action, for though they are normally quite helpful, they are sometimes of the Grin And Bear It disposition. Do not allow jackasses to force you out of a park. If the attendants won't respond to complaints quickly, phone the police. Rule 1 is: the farther a park is from a major center of population, the better it will probably be. Rule 2: the farther your site is from the toilets, the better. Rule 3: the farther back you are in the trees, the better (people want the least remote sites because of the bears, monsters, and so on.) Rule 4: if you're unhappy with the site assigned to you, go back to the park office and claim another. Throughout this book, I note the best places for camping.

As hinted earlier, the weather will often determine the direction your holiday will take. I have known summers when it was possible to camp out comfortably almost every night; but don't count on this. Some people of my acquaintance would not venture to come to Newfoundland without an RV or trailer, so that they don't have to sleep on the wet ground. But even with these, to keep your sanity you will occasionally have to go indoors, to either motels, hotels, or guest houses. Others among you will want to stay only in such establishments.

As in other provinces and countries, hotels vary tremendously in quality. They are also expensive; the Holiday Inn (466-7911) in Clarenville quotes a January, 1994, price of $75 per night for two people ("we don't know what it'll be in summer," I was told, but in summer, 1991, the rate was $96, and remember to add taxes of 20%). This for rather plain accommodation. The Mount Peyton Hotel (489-2251) in Grand

Falls and the Albatross Motel (256-3956) in Gander tend to be a little cheaper ($81, $62 respectively). I said cheaper, not cheap. The Glynmill Inn (634-5181), Corner Brook, quotes rates of $58-$76 (the hotel has old and new wings). Hotel Newfoundland (726-4980), Cavendish Square, St. John's, $128 (standard room), $165 (gold room); Radisson Plaza Hotel (739-6404), 120 New Gower, St. St. John's, $130; The Battery (576-0040), 100 Signal Hill Road, St. John's, $69, $79, and $89 (great view); Holiday Inn (722-0506), St. John's, $77 (including breakfast); the "best rate in town," Center City Motel (726-0092), 389 Elizabeth Avenue, St. John's, $39.99. Add taxes to these prices. Ask for special rates, weekend rates, or corporate rates. Check the competition: for example, in Corner Brook, the Mamateek (639-8901) and Journey's End (639-1980) motels may have the best rates in town. I always carry business cards and try to approach the reception desk with a swagger, as if I were a VIP. Hotels, I find, have lower rates for those who have (or seem to have) pots of money, and more expensive rates for the common joes like me and you.

As for guest homes, the provincial *Travel Guide* is useful; but take local advice and trust your own instincts. I also suggest you purchase or borrow *The Canadian Bed & Breakfast Guide*, by Gerda Pantel ($17.95), in its ninth edition (1993). Pantel recommends and gives detailed information on thirty bed and breakfast establishments in the following Newfoundland communities: Bay Roberts, Calvert, Cape Onion, Clarenville, Corner Brook (4), Cow Head, Daniel's Harbour, Eastport, Fogo, Fortune, L'Anse aux Meadows, Lewisporte, Norris Point, Port aux Basques, Roberts Arm, St. Barbe, St. John's (5), South Branch, Stephenville, Torbay, Trinity, Trouty, and Woody Point. Of course, this is but a fraction of the number of bed and breakfast establishments available on the island. A larger sampling is in the *Accommodations Guide*, published and distributed free by the Bed and Breakfast, Hospitality Homes, and Country Inns Association of Newfoundland & Labrador, Illiad Bldg., 280 Airport Blvd., Gander, A1V 1K6 (phone 256-4770). Generally, you can count on there being a b & b in larger communities. Gregarious people tend to like these places. I have not tended to frequent them ever since I stayed in "farm-houses" one summer in Ireland and ran into heated anti-Yankee sentiment (there being no distinction made between a Canadian, which in that setting I was quite happy to term myself, and an American).

Back to Port aux Basques, where you have been doubtless dropped at an ungodly hour by the Marine Atlantic ferry. (I have stayed here at St. Christopher's Hotel, $59, 695-7034). Now you can start off. You may if you choose take an immediate side trip on highway 470, along the south coast. This will give you a glimpse of outharbor life right away, in a setting, moreover, that you won't readily forget. Route 470 runs through a terrain of low hills, small, deep ponds, and struggling conifers or low brush, while offshore there is a menacing mix of rocks and sunkers, on which many a ship has come to grief. The land, obviously, is unsuitable for agriculture, if I can phrase it gently. Really, it is a skin of moss and growth over glaciated, rounded bedrock—not quite a typical headland scene, but you will note others in Newfoundland that will remind you of it. Most headlands on the island, exposed as they are to the brutal elements, have more than a passing resemblance to the Sea of Tranquility.

As you get farther from Port aux Basques on 470, the hills get bigger, the curves sharper. It is Newfoundland's answer to Italy's Amalfi Coast. Well, not quite.

The larger communities along this route—Isle aux Morts, Burnt Islands, Rose Blanche—seem prosperous, in sharp contrast to the niggardly setting. At Rose Blanche, note how well Newfoundlanders have learned to use every inch of space. Do not take your big trailer down into that community; you may not get it back up. But it is worth exploring.

Then, finally, Harbor Le Cou, a cosy little outport, one, moreover, that has been immortalized in a song about a seaman prone to adultery who spots a likely lass on the beach:

O boldly I asked her to walk on the sand,
She smiled like an angel and held out her hand;
So I buttoned me guernsey and hove way me chew,
In the dark rolling waters of Harbour Le Cou.

"Buttoned me guernsey and hove way me chew" has the authentic ring of a Newfoundland folksong. As you might already be able to tell, the sailor gets his comeuppance before the song is over. But I won't spoil it for you by giving away the ending.

Note the French element in placenames along this coast. The entire west coast of Newfoundland down to Cape Ray was once part of the French Shore, where, as already explained, the French could land and process fish until 1904. Newfoundland's first premier under Confederation, J.R. Smallwood, in one of his less lucid moments, proposed exporting Labrador hydro power, not through a corridor in Quebec, with which he was having a tiff, but across the Strait of Belle Isle, down the west coast, and across the Cabot Strait to Nova Scotia. French names everywhere. Smallwood called his suggested route "the Anglo-Saxon Route."

You are now ready to move north on the TCH. A word or two of caution. First, other drivers. Newfoundlanders are not the worst drivers in the world. (To say this would be to do an injustice to Neapolitans, who make a habit of driving the wrong way on one-way streets, Argentinians, and residents of certain of the more remote parts of Lapland who are accustomed to travelling by reindeer.) But they are close to the top of the list. Among their more amiable eccentricities are: 1. proceeding at a leisurely 80 kmh in a 90 or 100 kmh zone, then going like a bat out of hell on the inside lane in a passing area to prevent other drivers getting past them on the outside, *then* slamming the brakes on where the inside and passing lanes merge at the top of the hill—all this causing many a merry moment, and not a few heart attacks; 2. driving serenely out in front of fast-moving traffic approaching from a couple of hundred meters away, thereby forcing oncoming cars to squeal their brakes delightfully; 3. declining to pass slow traffic, therefore permitting a long build-up of snarling drivers; and much more. As you begin your journey on the TCH, prepare for a few near encounters with the Grim Reaper.

Also, beware of moose crossing the road, especially at night; if you hit one at high speed, you may well kill yourself and your passengers, not to mention the moose, for they are very big animals and for some reason seem to want to come near the highways at certain times of the year. Perhaps they just want an easy place to walk. Who knows? There is a big moose population in Newfoundland: slow down when you don't have a clear view. I'm serious about this. (Caribou are also a menace to drivers in some places, especially the southern Avalon.) And drive slowly in fog. Fog and moose are ubiquitous in Newfoundland. So are Mounties. Obey speed limits, although if you're in a hurry on a fog-free day you might get away with going 100 kmh in a 90 kmh zone, or 110 in a 100 kmh zone.

Just to come back to night driving. If possible, stay off the highways at night. I am not just thinking of the danger posed by moose and fog. The roads are hilly and typically have bad curves; in addition, highway construction projects are often poorly signposted. And in wet weather, which can't be avoided, older highways allow water build-up in truck ruts. This can cause hydroplaning.

As stated earlier, don't crawl along the highway. There is nothing more infuriating than to be stuck behind some lumbering RV, while the oblivious driver looks this way and that at the passing scene. Don't drink and drive. Penalties for drunk driving in Newfoundland are severe. Try to divine the most favorable times of the week and day for driving. Sundays on the TCH are hellish; in fact, weekends are. Try to limit your big moves to Monday, Tuesday, Wednesday, and Thursday. In some places, Bay Roberts and vicinity, for instance, on the Conception Bay Highway (route 70), traffic is *always* slow and excruciating, and there is nothing to be done but suffer through it. Again, on the TCH in the vicinity of Clarenville, traffic slows down to suit the inhabitants of the dozy little villages of Trinity Bay, who want to creep along at their accustomed 50 kmh. You will have much anguish there as well. Other spots offer the smart driver windows of opportunity. Don't try to exit from St. John's after 2 o'clock on a Friday afternoon in summer. Most government workers—and governments are the biggest employers in the capital—down tools and head for the bays around then. (On long weekends they start even earlier, around 11:00 a.m.) Driving in St. John's in summer, except on weekends when anybody thought to be worth his or her salt has skipped town, can be hectic. This may surprise you in view of the small size of the city. But every household in the yuppie parts of St. John's east has about four to seven cars—one for every member of the family, and possibly an extra four-wheel drive for Poppa. The big status symbol in those parts of town is the number of vehicles in the driveway. If little Johnny, at 17, doesn't get a Suzuki for Christmas, the neighbors might think his parents aren't millionaires.

In fact, hardly anybody walks in St. John's. To be seen carrying a bag of groceries up the street is a disgrace that will be talked about for hours at the golf club.

Come to St. John's, by all means. When all is said and done, it is the chief tourist attraction on the island. You can even camp there, in the Pippy Park Trailer Park towards the north of the city, which has tenting sites and picnic tables as well as hook-ups for RVs (Trailer Park registration: phone 737-3669), and stays open until the end of September. But come on Thursday, and stay through Saturday or Sunday, when, in summer, the town is deliciously empty.

To digress: the Trailer Park is adjacent to the Newfoundland Freshwater Resource Centre, which is a building through which trout swim. A lot of money has been spent on this. The fancy title is typical of names in The New Newfoundland. What used to be school board offices are now "Educational Complexes"; a hospital may be termed a "Health Science Centre" or "Community Health Centre." On occasion it is hard to tell what kind of institution you are entering. Sometimes you see the Far West summoned up in names: at the Mount Peyton Motel in Grand Falls, you may dine in the Peyton Corral; Baie Verte has a Chuckwagon restaurant; in St. John's you can have your whiskey straight-up in the Sundance Saloon; and from time to time you will find yourself driving on a "Trail." These names were inspired by J.R. Smallwood, a politician already alluded to, who once declared, I fear with no particular prescience, that "the cowboy looms larger in the future of Newfoundland than the fisherman." (Perhaps neither will loom large in Newfoundland's future.)

I will have more to say about names later. To return again to Port aux Basques. After leaving it on the TCH, you soon see the Long Range Mountains appear on your right, a massive presence across a broad meadowland. Two pyramid peaks rise before you. Beyond these, the ocean appears on the left, close to the highway, an inviting vista that stays with you until McDougall's Brook, whence you move inland and shortly are in the Codroy Valley. The mountains on the right will accompany you virtually all the way up the Great Northern Peninsula.

When I'm out west, I like to pop off on 408 to Cape Ray. Mind you, it is not a very imposing Cape, but there is a very good sandy beach nearby

The beach at Cape Ray.

which I have reason to contemplate with pleasure. Newfoundland is not blessed with a profusion of sandy beaches. Rocks and shingle are much more typical of the landwash. Not that I want to come down hard on beaches that aren't sandy. The pebbled beach has much to be said for it: you can pick up nice round rocks to heave in the water or at the cliff, the shellfish you find on it to roast won't have sand in them, and it roars nicely when there's a sea on, as the poet observed:

Come to the window, sweet is the night-air!
Only, from the long line of spray
Where the sea meets the moon-blanched land,
Listen! you hear the grating roar
Of pebbles which the waves draw back, and fling,
At their return, up the high strand,
Begin, and cease, and then again begin,
With tremulous cadence slow, and bring
The eternal note of sadness in.

Beach rocks don't have to make you melancholy, but they can. Their various colors—reddish sometimes, or exquisite shades of blue—can also make you cheerful. And if you are an amateur biologist, there's fun to be had exploring life-forms on the landwash: I recommend *Life on the Newfoundland Seashore: Seaweeds, Invertebrates and Fish*, by Michael Collins, $12.95.

At Tompkins and Doyles you are, of course, in the Codroy Valley, an agricultural region settled mainly by Scottish farmers from Cape Breton. It is not just one of the most attractive parts of Newfoundland; it is unlike anything else in the island that you will see. Take 406 from Doyles to Cape Anguille, perhaps stopping at Upper Ferry to get out of the car and consider the territory. This is the estuary of the Codroy, which here, so close to the sea, is a broad, slow, shallow river; mud flats and brackish marshes surround you; there are mountains on both sides, the Long Range and the Anguilles. You sense the slow pace and rituals of agricultural living. It looks a lot like the richer parts of the Maritimes, or even New England. (When I switched on the car radio, I heard the CBC from Sydney, which perhaps is suggestive.) Years ago at Cape Anguille—which is a community as well as a cape, again not an especially impressive cape but one I happen to like—I saw farmers baling hay, the first time I'd seen the process, though I've seen it often since then. Hay is still harvested out there, along with other products; cattle, sheep, and horses are in evidence. I don't know what you think; perhaps you're tired of seeing farm equipment come towards you on the road. But there is so little agriculture in Newfoundland, so little of the sleepy pastoral feeling of farmland, that I positively love dawdling in such a place as the Codroy Valley on a warm summer's day. Should you decide to stay for a while, camp at Grand Codroy provincial park, the best in the island for RV owners.

On the east coast, all the talk is of the fishery, with its torments and failures and subsidies and unions and battles. There is talk of it out here too, but not as much. Instead, on the radio someone is worrying about milk prices in Truro, Nova Scotia. A blessed relief.

I have to add that in the wonderful marshes of the Codroy estuary, and on the beaches and mud flats, birds abound. A birdwatching friend of mine who spent three days in this area in spring, 1991, saw 98 species, including great blue herons—somewhat uncommon in Newfoundland, although seen often on the beaches in PEI—six or seven species of ducks (the American widgeon was one), together with assorted warblers, thrushes, and vireos. If you have an interest in birds, be sure to take binoculars on your trip and Roger Tory Peterson's *A Field Guide to the Birds ... of Eastern and Central North America*, a paperback available in good bookshops for about $20. It has all the Newfoundland birds in it. Roger Burrows has written *Birding in Atlantic Canada: Newfoundland*, which gives a precise, area-by-area guide to the bird species he has seen. This is available from bookstores in Newfoundland for $16.95. But the Peterson *Field Guide*, in color, is of course better. Newfoundland has been described as a birdwatcher's paradise. Eastern seabirds abound: for instance, herring gulls and great black-backed gulls, gannets, Atlantic puffins, Leach's storm-petrels (Mother Carey's chickens), common murres and thick-billed murres (called turrs here), kittiwakes (tickleaces), guillemots, and razorbills. We also have the biggest bald eagle population in eastern North America, lots of osprey (fish-hawk), merlin (or pigeon hawk), goshawks, kestrels, boreal owls (with some great-horned and saw-whet owls), greater yellowlegs, snipe, sandpiper, grouse, etc. The 1989 field checklist of the birds of insular Newfoundland and its continental shelf waters, published by the Natural History Society of Newfoundland and Labrador (Box 1013, St. John's, A1C 5M3), lists some 343 species. At Big Barasway, just west of Burgeo, there are piping plovers, a threatened species. In 1991 only seven adults remained in the tiny colony; in 1993, there were thirteen, and others were found nesting at Grand Bay, near Port aux Basques, and (a pair) at the mouth of the Codroy River. Other threatened species occasionally seen here are the peregrine falcon and harlequin duck.

Talking of books, there are a few others I should mention right away, though I regret that as I write this one of them is out of print. It is Peter J. Scott's pamphlet called *Edible Fruits and Herbs of Newfoundland*, a valuable guide with a self-explanatory title. Obviously you will need to consult it in a library (or get Ryan's book—see below) if you intend to forage in the wilderness for food. Unless you have specialized knowledge—and I know that not a few of my readers who grew up in the '60s may have such knowledge—do not eat wild mushrooms (here often called fairy caps). At least two types of mushrooms that grow here, the fly amanita and the deadly amanita, are poisonous, and cooking them will not kill the poisons; they vary in color, but they have gills under the cap, a ringlike collar on the stem, and a cup at the base. For those who know what they are doing, chanterelles do grow here as well and of course are edible.

If in doubt, stick to berries. Blueberries, partridgeberries, bakeapples, raspberries, plumboys (a variety of raspberry), squash berries, strawberries, cranberries, crowberries, marshberries, gooseberries, and blackberries grow wild in Newfoundland. They ripen at different times in summer and fall. You will need to inquire about which ones are available, and where. By all means, go and pick as many as you want. Picking blueberries (August-September) and partridgeberries (September-November) is one of the most readily available delights of Newfoundland. They grow in vast quantities on the Avalon and Bonavista peninsulas, and elsewhere. Bakeapples, a choice, scarce berry, may be picked on marshes along the roadside from St. Stephen's to North Harbour on the southern Avalon, on the Great Northern Peninsula's bogs, and elsewhere from late July to mid-August. Watch for cars stopped by the side of the road; if you look away from the road, you will see people picking in the marshes. They won't mind if you go and pick near them. I mean the general vicinity, not on top of them!

On these marshes you will undoubtedly also see the crimson pitcher plant (or Indian cup), the floral emblem of Newfoundland. In the fall, they stand out beautifully. Don't haul one up to take back with you! It will die on the Canadian mainland!

The second book I want to bring in here is A. Glen Ryan's *Native Trees and Shrubs of Newfoundland and Labrador*, which is available free from the Parks Division, Department of Tourism and Culture (address on page 29). This is an excellent guide to the subject; it also lets you know what is edible, though Ryan's emphasis is different from Scott's, as the titles indicate. Neither Scott's nor Ryan's book is in color, which to my mind is a severe drawback. Again I have to mention a book in the Peterson Field Guide series: *A Field Guide to Trees and Shrubs (Northeastern and Central North America)*, by Petrides, readily available and invaluable.

The West Coast

I am suspicious of any stretch of coastline that is always called scenic in the tourist brochures, but the west coast of Newfoundland, from Cape Ray to Cape Bauld, is surely entitled to some such adjective. It is varied, sometimes flat, other times mountainous (by local standards), and, in the fiords of Gros Morne National Park, even nordic in character. I come from the Avalon Peninsula where, if truth be told, even the most charitable of observers will detect a certain sameness, at times amounting to monotony, in the scenery: always the short conifers, scrub, marsh, barrens, low rocky hills, and bare headlands. (Nor is that the only part of the island where one might, in passing, complain of a little ennui.) But in the west I feel as if I am in a separate country. For one thing, the climate is different from that in the east; it is warmer in summer, sunnier, better year-round. Farming country, as I've said, is a joy to behold on an island where there is so little of it; and I love seeing hills in the distance, even if they retain snow until depressingly late in the year. Many years ago, the first time I drove from Rocky Harbour to Plum Point and beyond, I recall seeing—I think just north of Daniel's Harbour—white sand being blown off the empty beaches across the road and through the trees, giving the landscape a magical, haunting quality. I now realize, having been back over the road a number of times since, that it was by no means a common sight. The road on the Great Northern Peninsula often strays close to the salt water's edge, which to me always seems to be what a proper Newfoundland road should do: I'd rather look at salt water than trees any day. The gloomy landscape in the vicinity of Eddies Cove East is also something to see. Many tourists happily remain on the west coast, and there is surely enough there to fill up a summer vacation.

St. George's Bay

Once you leave the Codroy Valley, I see no good reason why you shouldn't linger in the communities on the south of St. George's Bay. Let's say you turn off on 405 to Loch Leven and Highlands, then turn back up the coast to Robinsons and even Fishells. The communities are strung out as on a line, and indeed they were once on a line: the Newfoundland Railway, which must have been a very big factor in people's lives. One reason the patriots and dreamers of the 19th century gave for building the railway was to "open up" the agricultural resources of St. George's Bay. And so they were opened up; as opened up as they could be. Like the Codroy Valley, this is a farming region, though men also work in the woods for the big pulp and paper companies and at lobstering. I was impressed by the great level fields of hay, oats, and leafy vegetables at Highlands, and similar evidence of agriculture at Maidstone, where lines of white hay-bags were neatly arranged on the meadows. In Conception Bay, where I live for part of the year, there is little or no haymaking or any other kind of making. There *was*, during my childhood, in the 1940s and '50s; but not now. So I'm no longer used to seeing hay made, and I enjoy just sitting and watching people make it.

The coastline of St. George's Bay is flat and low, except for certain sections of Port au Port. Again, this is something I'm not used to, and it impressed me. To get to the narrow beach in, say, Highlands, you don't have to risk falling over a cliff, as you infallibly do in Conception Bay or the general vicinity of St. John's; you just stroll down a gentle bank. Well, it's not that easy, but you get my point. I did find my way to the beach, both at Highlands and, later, at Fishells. At the Highlands beach, while sitting quietly lunching on fresh strawberries, binoculars close by, I was rewarded by the sight of what I thought was a purple sandpiper. (There are plenty of sandpipers in Newfoundland, but the purple sandpiper is decidedly uncommon.) Fishells, at the end of a dirt road, turned out, unexpectedly after what I had seen, to be a fishing outpost, shacky and functional. There are places like this in Newfoundland—Long Point on the northern tip of the Port au Port Peninsula, Davis Cove on the Burin Peninsula, and Furby's Cove in Hermitage Bay are others—which offer a glimpse of what the primitive outport was like: the buildings on shore hurriedly thrown together, wholly secondary to the main business at hand, which went on in the boats far out to sea. (Alas, not a lot is going on out there now.)

A number of old houses along the coast here offer a reminder of the lives of the early settlers. I got out of the car and took photos of a couple of them; beneath the weathered and tattered exteriors, there was a hint—more than a hint—of elegance. I like the simplicity of old Newfoundland houses, the squareness of many of them, the sloping back linhays (or porches), the gently gabled roofs

House and crow, St. George's Bay.

(though many roofs, for example those in King's Cove, Bonavista Bay, or Harbour Grace, are steeply gabled), all of which to my eye are much better suited to the terrain than the new things people are putting up in an effort to be modern or postmodern, either the three-bedroom bungalow or, more recently, the dreaded yuppie house, all brown roof-shingle and angles, upstate New York stuff, horrid. I hope you like old houses too! I'm going to be going on a bit about them in this book. (To learn something about architecture in Newfoundland, look out for two books, each with drawings by Jean M. Ball: *A Gift of Heritage* and *Ten Historic Towns*, published in the 1970s by the Newfoundland Historic Trust, still occasionally seen for sale; and another by Gerald Pocius, *A Place to Belong*, which is available in most bookstores, though expensive—$55.)

May I turn now from houses to horses, which I saw again at Highlands and other places on this route? It is marvelous that horses, despite the advances in machinery and technological know-how, still perform useful roles in the working life of farmers and woodsmen. (See Andrew Fraser's book, *Founding Horses: The Working Horses and Their People in Canada's Past*, published in St. John's in 1991.) These peaceful, beautiful creatures have surely had a big part to play in ameliorating Newfoundland life over the centuries. I sometimes think they, along with other domestic animals, have done more in an indirect way to promote gentle feeling than the hundreds of missionaries did in their brazen, divisive proselytizing among the people—proselytizing that is still going on all over the island, but especially down north. It appears that to American evangelists in particular, Newfoundlanders remain sorely in need of conversion. They might be better advised to retail their spiritual wares around Detroit or East St. Louis. I see so many Mormons canvassing my neighborhood in St. John's that I've often been tempted to go to Salt Lake City to knock on doors and try to convert some of them; the trouble is I don't know what to convert them *to*.

But to come back to St. George's Bay. I was intrigued by the string of villages between Highlands and Fishells, so much so that I turned off again a little further along the TCH to Flat Bay and St. Teresa. Of interest on this road (apart from the gypsum quarry, one of the last mining ventures operating on the island) is the long spit of land shooting out from Flat Bay into St. George's Bay, offering great walking and beachcombing. I walked along it for an hour and found, among other articles, a stoppered bottle with no note in it, a fishing needle without the central spine that holds the twine, and three fairly intact heads of toy dolls. What is there in the heads of dolls that preserves them against the salt water?

The adventurer and writer William Cormack plunged down along Flat Bay Brook to the sea in early November, 1822, at the end of his pioneering walk across the island. There is now a community named after him, near Deer Lake. There aren't very many places named after writers in Newfoundland, though I have a good friend at Prowsetown, which is called after Judge Prowse.

Stephenville and Port au Port

Back, now, to the TCH. The first big town you will strike on your way north is Stephenville, which is best approached via route 490 through Stephenville Crossing. I like Stephenville a lot. Mysteriously advertising itself as the home of Canada's first international trade zone, it is a rough-looking place, sprawling, spacious, flat, not very busy, which nevertheless has the only annual summer festival of theatre on the island. In 1993 the Stephenville Festival (643-4982) had its fifteenth season; evidently, it's here to stay. Its principal venue is the main stage of the Arts and Culture Centre. It also has a Cabaret space, featuring folksinging, jazz, and other entertainment. The Festival, featuring professional theatre of a high caliber, takes place roughly from early July to early August. Stephenville is a good place to establish a headquarters for a few days. If you're bored with camping already, stay at my favorite hostelry there, White's Hotel (643-2101; $45 double early in 1994) on Main St. (the dining room, The Homemade Kitchen, is better than most restaurants outside St. John's)—or perhaps the newly opened Holiday Inn, $69, 643-6666—take in the theatre at night, and in the daytime head south for the beach at Black Bank Provincial Park, which has the warmest salt water I have found in Newfoundland. You can swim in it, and it is so shallow close in that children can safely splash around while you recline in the sun and read a good book. Maybe even one of my books! It is a long beach, narrow like all beaches in St. George's Bay, sandy, often kelpy, but acceptable.

Or you could head west from Stephenville to the Port au Port Peninsula, driving along 460 all the way to Cape St. George. Route 460 offers splendid views of St. George's Bay to the south; it is flat at the neck of the peninsula, but gets cliffier and more interesting as you approach the cape. Francophone visitors will want to stop along this shore to hear local French spoken (or choose the upper road, 463, to Mainland—La Grand' Terre—where you can take in the folk festival called Une Journee dans l'passe—a day in the past—held towards the end of July). Folk festivals here have a unique French ambience. The cape itself has been developed as a local park: Parc Boutte du Cap. It offers places to picnic, fresh water, some campsites, a playground for children, and so on. There's a festival out there too, Une Longue veillée—a long visit—held the first weekend in August; in 1994, the 5th-7th). An ugly steel fence near the cliff is supposed to keep drunks and children away from the cliff; but there is a gate through it. Go out to the cliff and look around. There's lots of room between the fence and the edge. But see that narrow neck of land, without sod cover, stretching out to the west? Don't walk out on that!

There's the bill of Cape St. George: one of the best things to see in Newfoundland.

The Bill of Cape St. George

To Burgeo

The road to Burgeo (480) is 150 km long: a very lonely drive. Sure you want to go on? The entire length is now paved, but it's a hard spot to get a flat or develop engine trouble. Backwoods campers will enjoy the road. A few good places to camp are found even in the early stages of the trip, because 480 stays close to Southwest Brook; and after you leave the Alpine northerly stretches—where you pass through a succession of high hills—you can pull off and get a good spot almost at will. (For information on the woods road that turns off to the northeast a third of the way down, see below, "Towards Buchans").

There is virtually no traffic on 480. You are passing through a part of the deep interior of the island only recently opened up to visitors, with little sign of human intrusion anywhere along the roadside until you get to Peter Stride's Lake. Flashing by is big timber with those skinny tops and then the black knob at the tip, as in a Tom Thomson painting. (This is close to pine marten country; the marten's existence is threatened because it likes big woods, and of course a lot of the forest in central Newfoundland has been cut by the paper companies.) As you get farther south, the hills give way to the familiar open barrens and low hills and marshes, though there are high hills in the distance. Look around you; it is great hunting and fishing territory. Great canoeing. An awful lot of bog. I have heard that one-seventh of Newfoundland is made up of bog.

Have you given any thought to bogs? I think I spent half my childhood up to my knees in them, even though they were regarded by the inhabitants of my community as just about useless. To the economist they perhaps *are* useless, except for the peat, which some on the southern Avalon and elsewhere have tried, not, I gather, very successfully, to use and market as fuel. But I wouldn't want to be one of those who badmouth bogs. They have their place in the structure of the good earth. They are wonderfully squishy to walk on. They are beloved of birds. Blue dragonflies that you can see through flit about on them. They are also full of wildflowers: irises, laurel, rosemary, butterwort, cotton grass, and bakeapple leaves. Not forgetting the pitcher plant! Marshberries and bakeapples appear in due season, of course. Brooks that wind their way through bogs are deep and menacing, with huge trout that allegedly are too cunning to get caught by a device so simple as a worm on a hook. If there's no wind, lie on your stomach by the side of one such brook, observe the queer things that hop over its surface, and look down at the slugs and other unsightly objects on the bottom. Reflect on all this. Wasn't it Melville who said that "meditation and bogwater are wedded forever"?

At Peter Stride's Lake, a lot of trailers have already been parked by hunters and weekenders. This is gravel-pit camping on a grand scale, and you can see that people take good care of their trailers and behave in a civilized way.

Here is a splendid, pristine lake. The last time I drove by, I stopped and ate lunch, swam, fished—no luck—then drank the lakewater without ill effect. Perhaps I should say at this point that you should feel at liberty to walk along the sides of rivers, ponds, and ocean in Newfoundland, and to swim and fish in them (subject to your having the required license). These are not owned by individuals, as they are, say, in New Brunswick and Scotland. They are common property.

At last, Burgeo, a community of about 3,000 people, punched out of a rock; or rather, clinging to a rock like a barnacle. It is compact, lively, and self-centered. Only recently released from isolation by the road, it has not yet overcome its surprise at being discovered. Offshore, the Burgeo Islands protect it from the open ocean. To the west, there is the gorgeous Sandbanks Provincial Park. There could be no better place to hang out for a couple of days. It is easily explored on foot; and, should you wish to take a boat trip, the islands in the distance seem very inviting. I regret to say there is a store termed the Dis and Dat Shop, but you can't have everything to your liking. The ferry to Ramea and Grey River offers the opportunity to look more closely at this dangerous, bleak coastline. It was likely off this coast that the sealing vessel *Southern Cross* was lost with all hands in the infamous spring of 1914, an incident recalled in a sorrowful Newfoundland ballad.

Burgeo has figured in recent Newfoundland history. In 1967 a large female finback whale stranded itself by pursuing bait fish into a deep saltwater pond near the community, and Farley Mowat, then a resident, turned the event into an international news story, which he later expanded into a book, *A Whale for the Killing*, now largely and deservedly forgotten. Five years later, the newly-formed Newfoundland Fish, Food and Allied Workers Union conducted a strike against the local fish merchant, which was widely regarded as an episode of great significance. Hence the bumper sticker "It started in Burgeo," which you can still see on some older automobiles. What is the "It," you ask? Hard to say.

Corner Brook and vicinity

Corner Brook is that rarity in Newfoundland: a town with a year-round industry, namely pulp and paper (although as I write this, early in 1994, the future of the mill once again looks uncertain). Depending on which way the wind is blowing, the sulfurous odor from the mill can be a deterrent to travellers. You will not often encounter this problem of industrial pollution in Newfoundland. Politicians and businessmen are, however, hard at work to get more of it here, and if you come back in ten years the place may smell like Hamilton.

Anyway, even if you don't sniff a fresh breeze as you get out of your car in Corner Brook, depend on it, the wind will soon change, so it's safe to stay for a while. The city has my favorite Newfoundland hotel: the Glynmill Inn, already mentioned. This is a somewhat old-fashioned establishment, but the rooms are comfortable, the main dining room is efficient and acceptable, the pub has a cosy atmosphere, and the Ewing Gallery is in the main foyer. In this gallery you will find the best of the painting that is done on the west coast, together with work by better-known townies or corner-boys (as residents of St. John's are sometimes testily referred to in Corner Brook). I have had some very pleasant stays in the Glynmill, except for one night when a convention of drunks kept half the hotel awake. Wild-eyed conference-goers are as much a menace in hotels on this mostly quiet island as in larger mainland centers. Which is one reason I tend to use a tent. If you are planning to stay in, say, the Mount Peyton Hotel in Grand Falls on a Saturday night, you might be well advised to ask if a wedding or convention is scheduled. If one is, avoid the hotel. You will get no sleep if you stay. To add just one more thing: if asked to choose between the old and new wings, I now choose the old. This is likely to be better built. In new wings, you can often hear what is going on in the adjoining room. "I don't care what you do," said Mrs. Patrick Campbell, "as long as you don't do it in the street and frighten the horses." Nowadays the horses might well be frightened if they passed innocently by some flimsily built new wings of Newfoundland hotels, and heard the sounds emanating therefrom.

But to the town. Corner Brook occupies a bowl-shaped setting at the head of Humber Arm, an inlet of the Bay of Islands. This bay is a deep fiord, ringed with high hills. There are few more striking natural settings in the island. It is a large city by Newfoundland standards (population: 25,000), and you will find in it the services you expect: good shopping, hospital, university, government offices, various banks, eateries, and so on. 13 West (at 13 West St.; 634-1300) is a fine, expensive restaurant. Find out what, if anything, is going on in the superbly equipped theatre at the School of Fine Arts in Sir Wilfred Grenfell College. As stated earlier, you can swim in the pool (637-2546) at the Arts and Culture Centre. If you come to Corner Brook in winter, ski at the Marble Mountain resort (639-8531; for Marble Mountain cabins, phone 634-2237). This mountain, a few miles down the Humber Valley, is unquestionably the best place to ski on the island.

The road south of Humber Arm to Lark Harbour (route 450) has scenery that resembles and rivals, but does not quite equal, that found south of Bonne Bay (route 431). The last time I drove to Bottle Cove, a beautiful, small, round cove at the very end of 450, I saw fishermen come in from the Gulf with their catches of very big cod, in the motor-driven dories that are characteristic of the west coast. Bottle Cove is a good place to start a hike. The Blow Me Down hills offer great views of the Bay of Islands. To the south are the Lewis Hills, which have the highest elevations in Newfoundland.

It was once said of Edinburgh that the best thing about it was the road that led to London. I intend no irony when I say that the TCH out of Corner Brook heading east along the Humber River is one of the finest things about that city. You descend quickly to the side of the Humber, which is a deep, fast-flowing river that always reminds me a bit of B.C.

rivers west of the Rockies. Then you proceed through the Humber Valley and along part of Deer Lake to Pasadena—an agricultural region, tastefully prepared for tourism, with campgrounds, vegetable, egg, and fruit stalls, u-pick strawberry farms, all very inviting. Deer Lake is on your left—one of Newfoundland's great lakes. The beach at Pasadena, where you might wish to spend an hour or so, is a bit rocky, but pleasing.

Old Prowse had been in the Codroy Valley and admired it, but, he said, it "is not comparable for a moment with the sylvan charms of either the Upper or Lower Humber." I'm not sure he would think the same today, since some of the "sylvan charms" have inevitably faded with the passing of the years. But it remains a beautiful part of the island.

Gros Morne

A national park in Canada is much more than a place to camp and frolic. It is a place to learn something about the flora, fauna, and rock structures of particular natural regions, ones thought to have something precious or unique that is worth preserving for future generations. Does this sound overly serious? Like a boring lecture? Sorry. But national parks really are outdoor classrooms of a kind, and if you miss what is being taught, well, the whole point of the exercise has rather escaped you. National parks are not family funlands. Don't expect them to be. Don't tell your children that's what they are.

Gros Morne is a wonderful park, and I suggest that before you visit it you should read something about what it has to offer. It offers an awful lot: boat tours of Western Brook Pond and Trout River Pond, 20 hiking trails varying in length and difficulty, including one (the James Callaghan Trail) to the top of the mountain Gros Morne (806 m), a number of campsites, including five "primitive" ones in remote regions that must be reserved in advance, places for rockclimbing, indoor and outdoor exhibits, interpretive events of various kinds, an old lighthouse to explore, restored fishing premises at Broom Point, beachcombing at Shallow Bay and elsewhere—or, rather, beach*walking*, since you are asked not to remove anything—and much more.

For hikers, what is called the "ultimate hiking challenge" is the 35 km trip to the eastern end of Western Brook Pond, for which pre-trip orientation is a requirement. This (with a backcountry permit) is obtained at the Visitor Center.

It is hard to absorb all this on a quick visit, and obviously it is wise to prepare in advance for what you want to do. For instance, the hike up the James Callaghan Trail takes approximately seven hours, so you must, a. be fit and, b. dress appropriately, bearing in mind that it can get very cold on a mountain. Ditto, if you take even the short hike to

Western Brook Pond, which is a must for those who want to see, from a great height, this beautiful, long, deep fiord-like body of water. So, write for information to: Gros Morne National Park, Box 130, Rocky Harbour, Nfld. A0K 4N0 (or phone 458-2417/2066). Ask specifically for *Tuckamore: A User's Guide to Gros Morne National Park* (published once a year, in summer), a pamphlet entitled *James Callaghan Trail*, which has lots of good stuff in it, and information about Western Brook Pond. A map of the park as well. All these are free. *Tuckamore* lists other books on the park for which you must pay.

You turn off the TCH near the town of Deer Lake onto route 430, the Viking Trail. The beginning of 430 is a kind of tourist strip, with farmers' markets, a "funland resort," ice-cream parlor, and so on. I normally turn west at Wintondale onto 431, which goes south of Bonne Bay, into Gros Morne, to Woody Point and Trout River. Note: if you take this route, you may well have to backtrack to Wintondale to get to the north part of the park, since the ferry from Woody Point to Norris Point, though marked on many maps, may not be operating. It did not operate in 1993. Don't count on it; make inquiries at Wiltondale, or by phoning the park office. Note too: if you want to get to the park's Visitor Center quickly, it is further along 430, before Rocky Harbour.

431—and 430 north of Bonne Bay—are just about the only roads on the island that can be called mountainous. About 10-15 km along on 431, you catch your first sight of Bonne Bay; soon afterwards you descend quickly into a deep valley, ears crackling as if in an airplane landing, down to Glenburnie, whence you proceed towards Woody Point along the bay. *Above* the bay, mostly; the livyers with houses between the road and

Bonne Bay, looking north.

the water often have to go down steep steps to get to them, which must be a lot of fun in winter. Wonderful views all along here; among the best Newfoundland has to offer.

Before getting to Woody Point, you turn left on 431 towards Trout River, remaining in Gros Morne all the while. Up, up goes the road, on what are known as Lookout Hills, offering great views of the mountainous terrain to the east and south. A few more kilometers and you find yourself in yet another deep valley, with extraordinary yellowish brown (in some light, red) hills on one side, grayish blue ones on the other. You soon come to a park exhibit site, where you might stop and consider the steep yellow hills close at hand. They are my notion of what the landscape of Hell is like: broken, bleak, eroded slopes, hostile to vegetation, without the green that signifies life:

... through many a dark and drearie Vale
They pass'd, and many a region dolorous,

as the poet says of the fallen angels. Actually, these Tablelands, as they are known, have their own weird beauty. Geologically, they are a wonder; they are peridotite, a dense rock thrust up many kilometers from their normal place deep in the earth's mantle by complex, primeval geological forces; they are some of the oldest rocks on the surface of the earth. Do you have an interest in geology? If you do, and are thinking of visiting Gros Morne, you should buy an exquisite little book called *Rocks Adrift: The Geology of Gros Morne National Park*, published by Parks Canada, and available for $10. This explains, and beautifully illustrates, the geology of the entire park, for there is much more of interest to the earth scientist in Gros Morne than the Tablelands. The layers of limestone and shale at Green Point (12 km north of Rocky Harbour; there is a campground nearby) and the limestone breccia cliffs at Cow Head, still farther north, are two other phenomena described in this book. And there is more. Believe me: it is worth the cash.

Back to the community of Trout River, with houses closely packed together, giving every indication of an intense community life—a once ramshackle, isolated outpost now suddenly dragged into the glare of publicity attendant on a national park, and sprucing itself up in an effort to be modern. This takes some doing. Here in 1990 I met a haycrate filled with hay, drawn by a sleepy old horse with bells on. I sped by in my Blazer, heading I

Haymaking, Trout River.

know not where, but the smiling man who was leading the horse was in no hurry to get to his destination: an interlude from ancient days. Trout River Pond, the southernmost camping and picnicking area of Gros Morne, offers excellent facilities. It is a splendid long pond, on which there is a Tablelands Boat Tour, which may be booked at Trout River (451-2101; 2.5 hours; $21.40, adults). The narrated tours both here and at Western Brook Pond (2.5 hours, $23, booked through the Ocean View Motel, Rocky Harbour, 458-2730), are concessions from park authorities; therefore the boats and services are of good quality. If you can choose only one, take the Western Brook Pond tour. To repeat: you *must* see that pond to get the full impact of Gros Morne.

Most of Gros Morne stretches north of Bonne Bay, but the part on the south of the bay should not be neglected.

Northward, however, we must go. If there's a ferry from the lovely village of Woody Point to Norris Point, take it. The scenery crossing Bonne Bay is simply glorious. From Norris Point, another striking community whose economy is tied to touring and other activities associated with the park, you drive to Rocky Harbour, which is, I guess, the commercial center for Gros Morne, with bustling and expanding services, one of which is a Recreation Centre with a 25-meter indoor swimming pool. You have to pay to use it. The community also has two restaurants good enough to make Anne Hardy's 1993 list of where to eat in Canada.

If the ferry is not operating, back to Wiltondale you go, and so on to Rocky Harbour.

The road between Rocky Harbour and Sally's Cove stays at times close to the sea, and you note the salt-stunted, wind-blown, twisted, flattened conifers at the ocean edge—called tuckamores or cronnicks—that are characteristic of this coast all the way to Eddies Cove East. These give ample testimony of the ferocity of the westerly winds that pound in off the Gulf in winter. Not to speak of the other seasons. If the trees have so much trouble in the struggle for life, what has it been like for men and women along the coast? These are a special breed of people. May I recommend a couple of books that do justice to them? One is *Beyond the Road: Portraits & Visions of Newfoundlanders*, by Stephen Taylor and Harold Horwood. It is out of print, but may well be in a library near you. Taylor's photographs are stunning; Horwood wrote the fine text. The second is E. Annie Proulx's splendid novel *The Shipping News*, for which the author won a National Book Award in the U.S.

Sally's Cove is famous for the role it played in the defeat of the Liberal premier J.R. Smallwood during the climactic general election of 1971, in which the Liberals won 20 seats, the Progressive Conservative opposition 21. However, St. Barbe, the district in which Sally's Cove was located, went P.C. by only 8 votes, and a judicial recount was ordered.

Much depended on the result. When the judge proceeded with his task, it was discovered that the Sally's Cove Returning Officer, Olive Payne, had burned her 106 ballots! Whereupon the judge awarded the district to the P.C.s, thereby hastening Smallwood's exit.

Sally's Cove has the typical look of communities along this road. There are few coves, as such. The houses have little protection from trees or hills; they just sit in a bunch on the flat, low coast, looking vulnerable and somewhat forlornly out of place. Not a lot of energy has gone into making these outports nice to look at.

You soon pass the path to Western Brook Pond, which I trust will not be one of the roads not taken in your life. Walk in to the pond and, if you're fit, take the path along the northern rim to Snug Harbour—an 8 km walk in total. Snug Harbour is on the pond; have a picnic there. Before getting to Snug Harbour, you have to walk over a suspension bridge. Courage! Want a shorter route? When you reach the pond, turn south. The end of this path is 5.5 km from the highway.

Before leaving Gros Morne on your way north, turn off and have a look at Cow Head: drive out on the causeway to "the head" itself, still the place where fishing is carried on, park, and explore the beaches. There is a lot to see out there. Near the end of the peninsula, should you make it that far, you will find grass to lie and sleep on—or to do whatever your heart desires.

Onward to L'Anse aux Meadows

The road north of Gros Morne passes through terrain that can be dismally barren and forbidding. That's how it appears to us today. But thousands of years ago, to people who first crossed the Strait of Belle Isle from Labrador to live on the island, it did not seem thus. These Maritime Archaic Indians lived by hunting and gathering; they had no agriculture. The Great Northern Peninsula, with its trees, seals, fish, birds, eggs, and berries, suited them just fine. At Port au Choix, on your way north, there is a now a National Historic Site devoted largely to these Amerindians. Until the discovery of an ancient cemetery at Port au Choix (dating from about 3,000 years ago) in the late 1960s, little was known about them; but when archaeologists uncovered and examined their tools, artwork, and weaponry, their important place in Newfoundland (and world) history was established beyond doubt. I say artwork: these people were far from being primitive savages. We always look back on early peoples and think them less than we are; but in many ways they may have been better than us, more finely adapted to their environment, with superior manual and other skills; smarter, perhaps even happier. One of the items at the Port au Choix Visitor Centre is a killer whale artifact, carved from igneous rock, which is exceptionally beautiful. If a sculptor produced it today, he or she would receive high praise from the sternest critics.

Like the Beothucks, who were likely their descendants, these Indians were expert at needlework as well as stone sculpture, using sewing needles carved out of the bones of birds. I recall the first time I saw a Beothuck child's moccasin at the Newfoundland Museum in St. John's, sewn with finely stitched deer sinew, which had been looted from a burial site in Notre Dame Bay in the 1880s. It was constructed with the greatest attention to detail. The child who wore it had been loved.

Out further on Point Riche—there is a 4 km hiking trail to the lighthouse—another archaeological dig uncovered materials relating to the Dorset Eskimos, who came to the area about 2,000 years after the Amerindians, stayed here (and elsewhere on the island) for hundreds of years, then disappeared from the archaeological record. These people too produced exquisitely crafted items, including carvings of bears. The Port au Choix area was a favored site for Beothucks as well.

Near Plum Point is the turnoff (432) for the remote outports of Main Brook and Englee. I have heard much praise of Tuckamore Lodge & Outfitters (address P.O. Box 100, Main Brook, Nfld. A0K 3N0; phone 865-6361), which operates a lodge a mile from the community, featuring such comforts as a hot tub and sauna.

On the road north to Eddies Cove East, you pass the ferry terminal at St. Barbe, to which you must go if you want to cross and see the remains of the 16th century Basque whaling station at Red Bay. Many visitors to Newfoundland center their vacations on Port au Choix and Red Bay.

But we will go on. The bleak, gray, exposed coast between Deadman's Cove and Eddies Cove East features flat shingle at the water's edge, tortured, stunted evergreens, low marshland off the road, and a spitting sea when the wind is onshore, smelling of old ocean, over which hungry gulls hover and scream.

Beyond Eddies Cove East, 430 turns east towards St. Anthony, the community that was the center of the mission founded by Dr. Wilfred Grenfell. Grenfell's name and muscular Christian spirit live on in the town. Read a bit about this great man, who left such an imprint on a region. You may wish to visit the Grenfell Museum, near the hospital. At the shop called Grenfell Handicrafts, across the road from the hospital, you can buy a striking Grenfell Parka, which is cut, sewn, and embroidered in St. Anthony, though the material is imported from England (1994 price, $228, plus GST); you can also get mitts, hooked rugs, travel bags, etc. Grenfell liked to parade his beliefs; look for the building bearing on its side the text "Faith, hope and love abide, but the greatest of these is love." It isn't often you see such a thing. The town and area repay exploration: you can stay at the Vinland Motel (454-8843; $67.50, double, plus tax); or, if you want to go along 437 to Cape Onion,

I recommend the Tickle Inn, "At the end of the Viking Trail," as the owners say (452-4321 in season, June to September, 739-5503 off season; $45-50 double, $40 single, plus tax), whose dining room was given a single star in Anne Hardy's 1993 *Where to Eat in Canada*—one of only two Newfoundland establishments thus honored.

Just southwest of L'Anse aux Meadows itself, in the open, rocky bay called Epaves Bay, you will find the reconstructed sodhouses of the old Norse settlement. It has been carbon-dated to approximately 1000 a.d.—the same date as that of Vinland (Wineland), the country described in the Norse *Sagas*, where Leif the Lucky founded a colony. Was Vinland Newfoundland? Not according to Parks Canada, because Vinland was a country, not a specific colony. Possibly the settlement at L'Anse aux Meadows was a stopping-off point to places farther south. We know such southern exploration took place because among the objects dug up by archaeologists at L'Anse aux Meadows was a butternut, and the northern limit of the butternut tree is northern New Brunswick. Leif the Lucky's men also found grapes at Vinland, or what they said or thought were grapes; and again the northernmost limit of wild grapes is New Brunswick. Does it really matter if this isn't Vinland? I couldn't care less. What matters is that the Vikings came here 500 years before Columbus, the alleged "discoverer" of America. They were highly skilled sailors, shipwrights, carpenters, and colonists. They smelted bog iron ore in a forge to make rivets and nails for their houses. Women sewed, knitted, spun, and cooked.

Reconstructed Norse sod huts, L'Anse aux Meadows.

It is impossible not to be moved by L'Anse aux Meadows. Wander around the bogland and drink in the atmosphere. When I last visited the site, these bogs were strewn with irises and other flowers. It is both a National Historic Park and a UNESCO World Heritage Site. One of the great things to see in Newfoundland.

Grand Lake

You have found your way back to the TCH at Deer Lake and turned east? Good. To reach Grand Lake, turn off at 401 and drive the 15 km or so to the little town of Howley. This is the only easy way to get to Newfoundland's biggest and most beautiful lake. On the way, you pass by a bit of Sandy Lake, which has become a touch shacky. At Howley you will find a private trailer park, from which you can launch your boat or canoe. (You can drive farther if you like, on a hydro road to the mouth of Hinds Brook, which flows into the lake.) A warning: Grand Lake is big, deep, and treacherous; if you are using a canoe, stay close to shore, and keep a wary eye on wind and waves. Remember that life-jacket.

It is simply a wonderful lake. I have camped for weeks at Whetstone Point, the vaguely defined "point" opposite Hinds Brook, whence I canoed, with companions, down and around exquisite Glover Island (an island with a pond that has six islands in it; those little islands are thus in a pond on an island in a pond on an island in the ocean), and took hikes inland from various locations, feeling all the while very much like the old explorers. The shores of the lake remain largely unspoiled; it is deep Newfoundland wilderness. Where the brooks flow into the lake there is often excellent fishing. If you are the type who wants to go off for a real wilderness holiday, this is the place for you. You will probably see wild animals (I saw two bears, moose, caribou, innumerable weasels—one of whom ventured into my sleeping bag—beaver, hares, and lynx); and be prepared to encounter deer flies. Always wear a good hat in the deep woods, because deer flies like to get in your hair and dig into the scalp, and it is a job to get them out. I saw lots of bats, too. Bats are a nocturnal animal attracted to movement, so if you are walking around at night outside a tent a bat might fly at your face or hair. Depending on your view of bats, this could cause slight tremors of excitement.

To repeat what I said earlier: the interior lakes of Newfoundland are open to all, even Gander Lake, which is the water supply for the town of Gander.

The Baie Verte Peninsula

Route 410, called the Dorset Trail, takes you to the Baie Verte Peninsula, a huge territory, sparsely populated, heavily wooded, and, if you like driving along the ocean rather than through interior landscapes, not especially inviting. Be prepared to drive long distances for such pleasures as the peninsula offers. But I had a good time poking around here and am much inclined to recommend it. Baie Verte itself, a substantial town whose fate was uneasily tied to the asbestos mine, is very welcoming of tourists. There is a bed-and-breakfast establishment called the Dorset Country Inn, $45, 532-8075/4293, run by the enterprising Bailey family. The main street has a couple of restaurants, one of which, Jim's, features Chinese food. I am not one for museums, but a Miners' Museum here (in the Baie Verte Economic Development Association Building) has information about various mines on the peninsula. There isn't much mining activity now. The asbestos mine itself, which remains the talk of everyone in the community, can be seen just north of the town on 410. It was a surface mine; hence you have left a desolate, gray hole, partly filled with water, and mountainous tailings. A wet reprocessing system is in place, extracting asbestos from the tailings; in February, 1994, this employed eighty people. Some are talking about the eventual use of the mine-site as an industrial dump.

You can tell from the homes and the general look of the town that Baie Verte has known prosperous times. But the mine manager's house was auctioned off a few years ago, china and furniture included, for a ridiculously low price. I heard one man say: "The future of Baie Verte is in the past." Yet hope lingers.

I stayed at Baie Verte and took the roads that spin off to the north, west, and east. The longest of these is 414, to La Scie, which not long ago was a bustling fishing community. From this route you can shoot off on dirt roads to Ming's Bight, Pacquet, and other places. It struck me in visiting La Scie and neighboring communities on the peninsula how many men up here (women too, no doubt) have kept up individual premises for fishing. This admirable practice is decidedly on the way out on the Avalon Peninsula, which doesn't mean the Avalon is more advanced, just more susceptible to trends. I found myself photographing the old finger-piers, with splitting tables or little fish houses at the end, secretly delighted to find many of them still in use and evidently thought to be efficient. With the cod moratorium in place, a lot of them can't be expected to last much longer, though some will be kept up for lobstering. The earliest surviving photographs of northern Newfoundland, dating from the 1850s, show premises like these. Let me be categorical on the matter: northern Newfoundland (from the Baie Verte peninsula east to

New World Island) is the best place to witness, and photograph, "old Newfoundland"—not only the skeletal remains that are seen in some other places, but still functioning units of fish production. Old, too, in another way: in some places up here you feel as if boats are just as important as cars in people's lives. Maybe more so. Some of the skiffs and dories, having outlived their usefulness, have been left outside homes and sheds as ornaments of a kind. I saw one dory that had been transmogrified into a flower bed.

At La Scie, I drove through the community and up a hill towards the CBC tower. Terrific view of White Bay and the Horse Islands. A smaller road leading towards the north bill of Cape St. John looked very inviting.

To mention two of the places you might go, off 414. Shoe Cove, just south of La Scie, is a bowl of a community with a concentration of houses and activity in the narrow slit that leads to the ocean. Through this slit you drive to find a wharf. Here I took photos of houses built out on the side of cliffs.

At Shoe Cove, near La Scie.

Tilt Cove is an astonishing place. It has to be seen to be believed. Once a prosperous copper-mining town with a population of 2,200—it had more people than Placentia and Brigus in 1905—it now has around eight families, many of them seniors. The mine closed for good in 1966. It is another bowl-shaped place, but it looks derelict and forlorn and ravaged, as if scooped out of the surrounding cliffs by giant machines. In fact, it has the futuristic appearance of a blasted earth. Car wrecks stick out of the muddy central pond. Out near the wharf the rotting skeletons of an immense shed and conveyor belt bear witness to what it once was. The wharf too, designed to accommodate huge ships, is grimly crumbling. It was of no use to the one fisherman left at Tilt Cove in 1992, who fished from the beach as his ancestors may have done over a century ago. A spectral community.

After returning to 410, you might go and see Wild Cove in the west, on the shores of White Bay. This is a little cove at the foot of very high hills. I regret to say that on the road down to it there is a big garbage dump, visible and offputting. The cove itself has two sides: the old and the new. The new has a fish plant, the old has premises, somewhat in decay, in the traditional style. I naturally preferred the old part, in which there was a church which had its roof blown off, perhaps the act of an angry God who had tuned in to the latest ecclesiastical news from Newfoundland. However, people had been at work putting the roof back on. It was at Wild Cove that I got my first sight of the lower half of White Bay, and resolved to explore it more fully in the years ahead. On the northern side of the cove, through the fish plant's yard, a wooden walkway leads to an inviting headland picnic site.

Finally, north to the communities of Coachman's Cove and Fleur de Lys, which is where the Dorset Trail ends. At Fleurs de Lys, we see where

Abandoned fish-house, Fleur de Lys.

the name of the "trail" comes from. There is a quarry here, from which the Dorset Eskimo and (possibly) the Maritime Archaic Indians cut soapstone blocks from which pots, lamps, and other artifacts were gouged. The site does not seem well looked after. It overlooks the older part of the community, with stages and sheds toppling into ruins. The other side of Fleurs de Lys is more active and modern. Here, next to a modern bungalow, I saw an old-fashioned, one-cylinder, inboard gasoline engine that had been painted blue and stuck up on a rock as an ornament. Engines like these, going by such trade names as Acadia, Atlantic, and Coaker, were critical to the inshore fishery from the 1920s to the '50s. One of the sharpest memories from my

Engine, Fleur de Lys.

childhood is of hearing their unmistakable putt-putt as the skiffs headed offshore to the cod-trawls early in the morning. While the skiff has not been abandoned, the peculiar old sound is now a thing of the past; the engines, yard art. *Sic transit gloria mundi.*

Not that I wish to denigrate yard art. In fact, I like the way Newfoundlanders make use of discarded objects such as engines, wooden wheelbarrows, box-cart wheels, carriages, and so on, on their front lawns. It shows a reluctance to let go of the old ways.

Coachman's Cove is broad and exposed, with twisted formations of jade-like bedrock. I had been told by a friend to investigate the graveyard here, and indeed it is well worth a visit. The headstone of Frenchman John Marie Le Mee, with those of his wife and daughter, is a reminder of the links between this coastline and France—for we have not yet left the old French Shore, and memories are long:

> On cold days now, when the wind is in
> and the shore sand taps my window pane,
> I close my eyes
> to see them moving in the landwash still,

as the poet Tom Dawe writes. It is an old place, Coachman's Cove, reminiscent somewhat of Conception Bay outports of forty years ago. In finding my way to the cemetery, I was pleased to have to drive under a wooden walkway between a flake and a fish-house. The congested landwash brought back memories of days, not very distant, when every foot of land near the water was used in the processing and drying of fish, and when a boy sent to do a message for his father on a beach might find that, although it was a sunny day above, he was walking half the time as if benighted, under fish-flakes loaded with drying cod.

At Coachman's Cove.

Green Bay

Back on the TCH, you come next to the road to Green Bay (really an inlet of Notre Dame Bay), which advertises itself in brochures and on highway signs as "scenic." Indeed it is a beautiful bay. I like bays where you can see across to the other side, hence giving the impression that you really are in a bay: this is such a one. I took 391, the road to King's Point and Rattling Brook, where I'd been told there was indeed a brook that rattled in spectacular fashion. Luckily for me, the day before I went to hear the rattle it had rained heavily. Hence the brook toppled off the high hill behind the community in great style. I found both King's Point and Rattling Brook to my liking, the latter very much so. The view here is a mini-version of that in Bonne Bay; the place has a relaxed, pastoral quality, nestled as it is at the foot of what is termed locally, and not without reason, a mountain. There is a hiking trail up that mountain. Would that I was in good enough shape to tackle it. Agriculture and poultry-farming are carried on here, but until recently fishing remained a

Outhouse, Rattling Brook.

big part of the economy. I loved seeing a venerable fish-house that had been kept upright—or at least prevented from falling over—by shores; while nearby an old-fashioned, hand-crafted skiff, of a type still in use in northern bays though giving way steadily to fibreglass 20-footers, had been sawed in half, and the bow upturned, fitted with a doorway, and used as a toilet! Here's a man who not only forbore to part with his old skiff but made it a part, nay, a vital part, of his private and contemplative moments. Is he the mayor of Rattling Brook? I hope so.

The Beothuck Trail

Route 380, called, for some reason, the "Beothuck Trail," turns off at South Brook. You should take this if you want to see the charming outport Pilley's Island, which has been written about so well by essayist Cyril Poole. Actually it is no longer an island, since it is connected at two points by causeways. Pilley's Island and, later on, the bigger community of Triton (pop. 1,300), afford glimpses of islands and arms in Notre Dame

Bay; it is a bay of quite appealing inlets, islands, and long narrow capes. You get an impression of cosiness in these parts. The sea seems to lose its ferocity in the little sheltered inlets; the great, fearsome expanses, stretching off into nothingness at the horizon, often aren't visible. Houses often sit right at the edge of the sea, instead of staying well away from it, as they do in more exposed harbors. Boats are moored close to shore, as if no wave could come along to pitch them onto the rocks.

There is a dirt road across Pilley's Island to a ferry terminal, where you can take a very cheap ride to Long Island and Little Bay Islands.

Triton and Robert's Arm are biggish places with services for visitors. In Triton, I saw fresh squid advertised and, it being a rainy day, went to a restaurant to try some. It was called the Beothuck Restaurant; on the wall were displayed a reproduction of Lady Hamilton's lovely picture of the Beothuck Demasduit (called by the English Mary March), who was captured in March, 1819, in a bloody episode on Red Indian Lake which saw her husband and possibly another male Indian slaughtered; and a "Newfie" three-dollar bill! The tragic and pathetic Newfoundlands, side by side. The only way squid was served, I regret to say, was in deep-fried rings, which gave a good taste of the batter and very little taste of the squid. Newfoundlanders do not know how to cook squid. They discard the tentacles—which are delicious—and hardly know what to do with the sheath of meat that covers the guts.

Towards Buchans

The road from Badger to Buchans and Millertown (370) is, though paved, very rough in places. It is worth taking if you want a glimpse of the interior woods and lakes, and especially if you want to go canoeing. The Exploits River flows near the road in the early stages of the trip south and is readily accessible. At Mary March Provincial Park, supposedly built on the site of a Beothuck encampment, you can easily carry your canoe to the rough shoreline of Red Indian Lake, cluttered here with logs and debris. The lake at this point is shallow and uninteresting; in fact, it is somewhat shallow throughout its length, and I don't think is particularly good for fishing. Still, it seemed inviting. The last time I was in Mary March Park was on a Labor Day weekend. Nobody was camping or picnicking there.

The 19th-century writer Philip Tocque wrote of Red Indian Lake that in a hundred years steam-boats and yachts would be darting to and fro, unloading merrymakers, filling warehouses. That time is still a good ways off.

It is now possible to drive from Millertown on an Abitibi-Price woods road south of Red Indian Lake, take the bridge across Lloyd's River, and connect to the Burgeo road (480). (A very rough road north of the Lake from near Buchans is kept open by hunters but is not recommended.) Proceed at your own risk; you would be well advised to use a four-wheel drive vehicle, bearing in mind that Abitibi-Price tractor-trailers use the road year-round to supply its mills with wood. For information on this particular road, phone Abitibi-Price in Stephenville: 643-7512. Abitibi-Price, which has pulp and paper mills in Stephenville and Grand Falls, and Corner Brook Pulp and Paper in Corner Brook, own and operate woods roads which, within certain constraints, are open to the general public and offer access to wilderness. These are marked on the provincial government highway map with thin black lines. If you have questions about particular roads, you should make inquiries directly to the woods departments of the two companies: Abitibi-Price, Grand Falls (292-3000); Corner Brook Pulp and Paper, Corner Brook (637-3000).

Grand Falls

The town is now officially and clumsily called Grand Falls-Windsor. It dates from 1905, when construction began on the pulp and paper mill at the falls on the Exploits River. Grand Falls is said to be the first Newfoundland town to be built out of sight and sound of the sea. The initial owners and operators of the mill were the English Harmsworth family, which retained control until the early '60s; hence there was something English about the town from the beginning, and there is something English about it yet. There was, for instance, an English-style stately home near the town, to which only the best people were invited. A Grand Falls Club was set up in 1911. A park in the center of town has a passing resemblance to parts of Primrose Hill in London, and a horse show is held annually. Horticultural shows were held as early as the 1920s, during which hungry decade thousands of Newfoundlanders were fleeing the poverty of the outports to settle in foreign places such as Massachusetts and Nova Scotia. But the company town of Grand Falls remained prosperous even through the Great Depression. It has always regarded itself as a cut above most Newfoundland communities.

It is a terribly nice place to walk in and stay in. High Street (note the English resonance) and Main Street have shops and services; you can go on a tour of the Abitibi-Price mill in the summer months; there is a Mary March Museum focusing on the unfortunate Beothuck. Nearby Beothuck Provincial Park has a replica of an old logging camp, which gives some sense of what life was like for the loggers and drivers on whose labor the prosperity of Grand Falls was based. Missing, however, are the cold beans and hard tack.

North of Botwood

Botwood, a substantial town, is a port through which the Abitibi-Price mill in Grand Falls ships its products. It played a role in the history of aviation in Newfoundland, and you will find an old water-bomber, its days of bombing forest fires over, on display near the docks. In 1991 I was surprised to find the venerable coastal steamer, the *Terra Nova*, tied up here. Inquiries disclosed she had been tied up for over a year because the owners had found no work for her to do. She was subsequently sold, and I can report she now sails, though under a new name, from Tampa to Caribbean ports, carrying freight through far warmer waters and sunnier climes than those of Notre Dame Bay. She escaped the fate of the *Kyle* in Harbour Grace, once a graceful ship, the pride of her time, now an ugly, rotting hulk sitting, hove to one side, on the bottom out in the middle of the harbor.

Route 352 from Northern Arm stays near the low coastline of the Bay of Exploits, and is lined with ocean-front cottages. The last time I passed by here, the trees had just been touched by the first frosts, and the colors of the leaves were impressive, with bright reds standing out sharply from the mostly green backdrop. It's trite to praise autumn colors, but well they might be praised! At any rate, they never cease to delight me. On a sunny fall day, you wonder why people want to come to Newfoundland in summer. Next day, when you get a driving, cold rain, you wonder why you wondered.

On to Fortune Harbour, a big, snug harbor well out of the reach of ocean waves, ringed by high hills, quite picturesque. In fact, you can't see the harbor entrance from the shore, and I'm told a novice sailor will have trouble finding his way to the open sea. This is an old place, with an impressive number of crumbling houses that speak of more prosperous times, although there is a mussel processing plant and, every year around the end of July, a Mussel Festival that attracts a lot of visitors. (I bought a bottle of local mussels at a convenience store; they were delicious.) Mussels are now a big factor in the economy of northern Newfoundland, and you will often see lines of blue mussel floats in the harbors. These are really apple juice barrels. Newfoundland fishermen are adept at converting plastic containers such as these barrels and Javex bleach bottles into usable buoys and other kinds of gear.

There are many traces of modernity here, but the main impression is of age and remoteness. I again had the feeling I keep having in the island's northern reaches, that of stepping back in time. One old house had an antique green settle on its verandah, "placed for ornament and use," as the poet says. St. Anne's Church has to be at least a hundred years old. I saw a number of things here I had never seen before, among them an old skiff, at anchor, with a scarecrow at midships to keep the gulls away, and a mailbox made out of a five-gallon beef bucket!

Back at Northern Arm, you might turn north through Point Leamington to Leading Tickles, a community (pop. 650) spread out in untidy fashion around an inlet, with houses hugging the seashore in the old style. The road circles above the community, so you have to get out of the car and find your way through narrow lanes to the shoreline in order to get the full flavor. People either make a living on the salt water or else cut and

Mailbox, Fortune Harbour.

thin timber for Abitibi-Price. No notion of prettiness here, but signs of vitality and determination. Cod is no longer king in these parts; instead, squid is big. I saw many racks covered with squid-lines heavy with drying

Squid-lines, Leading Tickles.

fish. On a beach I found and photographed a battered boat that had been left to rot. I have to say that it was not an odorous or pleasant stretch of beach, for the ocean is still regarded by too many Newfoundlanders as a place to toss debris. In Leading Tickles and nearby Glovers Harbour you see rough and ready northern outports, indifferent to tourism and untouched by it, getting on with business. Don't look for family funlands in such places; but you might get instead a true taste of Newfoundland.

In some cliffy areas of Newfoundland you have trouble finding a place to launch your boat, but on the roads north of Botwood you can do so with ease. This is a low-lying region, with great arms of the sea penetrating the land, and there are many inviting spots to go boating. Indeed, the whole of Notre Dame Bay seems ideal for sailing and boating.

South on the Bay d'Espoir Highway

Route 360 takes you through the central wilderness to a remote and economically precarious part of the island. The road has no services until you reach Bay d'Espoir (pronounced despair) 130 km away, so gas up and check your tires before attempting it. You pass through rough cutover and burnt-over timberland in the northern stretches. Halfway to Bay d'Espoir, the highway crosses the Northwest Gander, a river eminently suitable for canoeing and very inviting. Further south, the forest becomes less ravaged and the familiar high conifers and birches of central Newfoundland make their appearance. The speed limit is a ludicrous 80 kmh, and I suggest you stay close to it: the RCMP on the south coast, as in other remote parts, have little to do except ticket unwary motorists.

Route 361 goes around the head of Bay d'Espoir to St. Alban's. At the community called Head of Bay d'Espoir there are two motels, the Vancor Motel and Motel Bay d'Espoir; back on 360 there is a provincial park, the only one in the region; so there are places to stay if you want to go fishing or boating. These are the chief tourist attractions of the area around the head of Bay d'Espoir, though the scenery is also striking on this deep fiord-like bay. Near St. Veronica's there is good steelhead (sea-run rainbow) fishing; these fish are escapees from the sea-pens in nearby Roti Bay, which are owned by the SCB Fisheries hatchery. Ask locally where the best fishing is. The hydro road inland from St. Veronica's leads to the Bay d'Espoir reservoir, where there are brook trout and ouananiche.

By all means go to St. Alban's and poke around. It is a large community; there is little in the way of a fishing industry, or for that matter any kind of industry. It does not have a prosperous look. However, the size of the local ecclesiastical establishment suggests that the church at least has done well. Tourism may be the future around here. If not, what future does it have? A marina has been built to accommodate yachtsmen who might choose to sail up Bay d'Espoir, and boats may be hired to tour around the islands and crannies of the bay.

Let's head back to 360 and head further south (stopping, first, to visit Conne River, home of Newfoundland's Micmac Indians). The road soon rises to a plateau; the big trees disappear; you see around you an expanse of unspoiled open country, with low hills, pristine ponds, brooks, marshes, and scrub. This persists all the way south to 362; and along 362 (now paved) to English Harbour West in Fortune Bay, except that on this latter road the hills are higher, the vistas even more impressive. The country commands such views that in fall hunters often don't bother leaving the road to kill their moose; they drive up and down the highway in their pick-ups, and wait for the unlucky moose, spotted far off in the treeless wild, to find their way to the road. A bit like shooting fish in a barrel. A *lot* like it.

At English Harbour West I recommend you stay at the Olde Oven Inn (888-3461/3456; $50, plus RST, double, bed and breakfast; a three-course dinner for $20), a home in traditional Newfoundland style, tastefully preserved, very comfortable. The community itself is small and charming, strung along shore in a snug semicircle at the foot of a high hill. Just offshore is English Harbour Island, a natural breakwater. I saw three old wooden windlass-style winches, of a kind I thought long extinct, but still in use here. On both sides of the harbor are headlands where you can hike (not without some danger from broken beer bottles), or just sit and look out over Fortune Bay. J. Petite & Sons, owners of the Olde Oven Inn, will arrange boat trips around the bay, even as far out as resettled Sagona Island.

From English Harbour West you will want to take trips west to Boxey and Mose Ambrose, and east to St. Jacques and Belleoram. Yarn Point Knitters at Mose Ambrose has excellent, moderately priced, woolen knitwear. The road from St. Jacques to Belleoram rises to a great height, offering views of the Burin Peninsula in the distance, Fortune Bay itself, and islands in Belle Bay near at hand. Do not miss making this short journey if you are down this way.

Winch, *English Harbour West.*

Headstone, English Harbour West

It is full of drama. The plunge down to the closely packed, raggedy town of Belleoram is also memorable.

Very shortly after turning left off 362 onto 360, you see Hermitage Bay in the distance on the right. You catch better views of it as you head further south on 360 and turn off on 364 towards Furby's Cove. (Now you see Connaigre Bay as well.) These are roads at high altitude. Hermitage Bay is a narrow, deep bay, with high cliffs on both sides, but especially on the west side. No one lives year-round in this bay north of Hermitage and Gaultois; there are a few summer cabins on the east side, but only one place before Furby's Cove where you can get access by automobile to the water's edge. Thus it is virtually an unspoiled wilderness. It looks a lot like parts of Western Brook Pond in Gros Morne; some might even prefer it, since it is perfectly natural, without walks, guides, and so on. I think it is one of the great beauty spots of Newfoundland.

Go down to Furby's Cove and have a closer look. There are few, if any, year-round liveyers in Furby's Cove, but people from Hermitage live there in summer and fall. Hire a boat for an hour or two to take you northeast into the secret recesses of the bay, perhaps to watch for eagles (which are commonly seen, especially in early morning, along the cliffs on either side). What should you pay for such an expedition? I'd say $40-$50 per hour is a reasonable price. The cliffs are stunning to look at; so high and precipitous on the west that it is next to impossible to harvest the wood that grows on them; along the eastern side can be seen shallow coves—coves with names—from which one or two families fished in obscurity decades ago. Beaches are scarce; the few you see are narrow. This is such a deep bay that a few yards offshore the cod-jigger goes down—used to go down!—twenty or thirty fathoms. In the middle, I was told, it descends to two hundred fathoms or more.

Drive on to Hermitage (from which the ferry leaves for Gaultois) and beyond. A rundown municipal park at Hermitage, located behind an attractive barasway, represents a perfunctory gesture towards tourists. From Hermitage to Sandyville (or Dawson's Cove, as it used to be called

Fish flake, Sandyville.

and perhaps should still be called) there are marvelous views of ocean and distant coastline. At Sandyville you come down to the flat, low coast. Sandyville is worth stopping at. The central beachy area where some fishing is still carried on was the site of the original community, but people have now moved back to the sides of the highroad in their bungalows. Out on the original site I saw (in 1991) an old fish-flake made of longers, once a common sight in Newfoundland outports, now, alas, rare. In the grass near the flake are abandoned concrete steps and foundations of old houses. As the name implies, there really is a sandy beach.

From Sandyville to Seal Cove the coast is low and marshy; brooks and barasways catch your eye; the road stays close to the salt water. Great birdwatching country. At Seal Cove you are at the end of settlement on this peninsula, but do go on over the primitive, wild track that leads towards Pass Island. I have talked of remoteness: this setting *is* remote. You want isolation? Here it is. The track ends at a wharf where you can stand and look across a narrow channel to the island itself, now resettled, once a vibrant fishing community. It is said that Ted Russell, the Newfoundland author, modelled his imaginary outport of Pigeon Inlet on this place. (Note: the initials are the same.) Take out your binoculars. Look over there. Carefully, or you will miss it: a cemetery in a shallow valley, wherein lie the abandoned dead of Pass Island:

Far from the madding crowd's ignoble strife,
Their sober wishes never learn'd to stray;
Along the cool sequester'd vale of life,
They kept the noiseless tenor of their way.

Back on 360 proceed south over high rolling hills to Harbour Breton, which is the service center for this entire peninsula. Maybe you'll want to stay a while. This is a modern community (pop. 2,400), with hospital, drug store, motel, etc. I looked for the old premises of Newman & Co., the biggest merchants on the south coast in the 19th century. I was told they had been torn down. Pity.

Lewisporte and vicinity

North again, to the TCH. Lewisporte is a busy, progressive place, with good services for tourists—a town where you might well pause for a day or two and shoot off along roads to the west, north, and east. Then you can head north to Labrador. A Marine Atlantic ferry, the *Sir Robert Bond*, runs from Lewisporte to Cartwright and Goose Bay in Labrador (June to September; reservations 772-7701; one-way adult fare to Cartwright $53; to Goose Bay $85; automobile to Goose Bay, $140; rates as of

February, 1994). In addition, in the summer of 1993 Marine Atlantic started a "Northern Cruise" between Lewisporte and Nain (in Labrador), using the *Northern Ranger*. The round trip takes some 17 days (calls are made at various points en route) and is expensive, but an artist friend of mine who took it described it as "unforgettable." In 1994, Marine Atlantic may use the *Taverner* as well as the *Ranger* on this run. For information on rates, cabins, etc., phone 695-7081/7082, or write: Reservation Bureau, Marine Atlantic Inc., P.O. Box 520, Port aux Basques, Nfld. A0M 1CO. Ask for the pamphlet *Cruising Labrador*.

Route 341 southwest of Lewisporte through Stanhope and Brown's Arm offers distant ocean views of small, rounded, wooded islands—like a third of an egg protruding above the water, very enticing. You will also see obtrusive evangelical signposts along this road, which may please or disconcert, depending on your own beliefs. One bearing the unequivocal message "Holiness Or Hell" gave me, I must say, food for thought.

Laurenceton, located on a gorgeous inlet of the Bay of Exploits, is a mixture of old and new, with some houses dating perhaps from the turn of the century, now abandoned, indeed in an advanced state of decay, but lovely to look at. I mentioned earlier how junks of wood, pieces of fishing gear, etc., are often so roughly thrown together outside outport homes that the dainty eye is offended. But you will also see the opposite of this: lobster pots and graplins stacked just so, logs and woodpiles too, and much else that shows neatness at least, if not an aesthetic sense. As fall approaches, roadside heaps of birch and spruce junks are found all over northern Newfoundland. Here at Laurenceton I saw one such huge pile that had been spread over a granite outcrop, but in a way that was both efficient and tidy—truly, yard art.

Woodpile, Laurenceton.

Route 342 goes north from Lewisporte to Embree and Little Burnt Bay, the latter a pretty little harbor with flat rounded rocks—sunkers—out in it, and more around the sides of it. Great views of offshore islands on this route. The road goes close to the sea, and with an onshore wind and just middling waves I could observe how vulnerable the various premises and moored boats were. In fact, I myself was not beyond the ocean's reach, for at one point a few drops of salt water splashed over my windshield and, since I had the window open, over me— the "spit of the sea," as Duley put it. It was good once more to see the old-fashioned skiff still in use. As already suggested, you run into ruins of such boats too all along the northern coastlines. Just outside Embree I found one that was being sawed into usable junks by a thrifty young man, and managed to get a few photos of the skeleton before it too was made ready for the flames.

On the road from Lewisporte to Campbellton (340), you pass the Notre Dame Rod and Gun Club, to which visitors have access on request. This is a touristy road, with mini-golf, a farmer's market,

Skeleton, near Embree.

Scene, near Lewisporte.

and a picnic area near the bones of an old pulp mill, a melancholy sight which some might say is a symbol of Newfoundland industrial development; the views of the ocean are lovely. Turn off on 343 to Newstead and Comfort Cove, which are at the end of a short peninsula. At first you encounter houses of glossy newness, but as you move on the old asserts itself. At Newstead there is a bird sanctuary in a salt water marsh, a good spot to spend an hour or so with binoculars. I was richly rewarded for my own stay near the marsh. The fishery in these places, as in so many others, is virtually defunct, and I saw assorted premises in a bad state of repair. At the end of one wharf that had been wrenched into an almost snake-like posture by winter ice, a fish-house had tilted perilously, and seemed about to slip off its place and float out to sea.

Scene at Newstead.

The Road to the Isles

Let us jump now to the northerly end of 340 to what used to be Chapel Island and Cottle's Island and New World Island and Twillingate Islands but which is now, owing to causeways, an extension of the mainland. Not that you won't sometimes feel you're on a remote island when travelling out this way; you certainly do feel that. At times, too, for example when approaching Summerford, you run into houses and lawns that are as urban-looking as Etobicoke. This is a region of contrasts; a dramatic and spectacular part of Newfoundland, a must to see. Note: it is one of the driest regions in the island; I saw no lounges or bars north of Boyd's Cove.

There are a lot of communities out here, but apart from Twillingate there were two I especially wanted to visit: Moreton's Harbour and Herring Neck. To get to Moreton's Harbour, you turn northwest on 345 at Virgin Arm. I wanted to see this place for two reasons: first, it is associated with—but not called after—the 19th century English missionary Julian Moreton, who wrote an odd book, one I like very much, about his experiences in Newfoundland; second, the poet E.J. Pratt taught school here and it undoubtedly left a mark on his sensibility. Though I don't care for a lot of Pratt's work, some of his early lyrics inspired by Newfoundland are classic pieces.

I was much taken with Moreton's Harbour and spent most of an afternoon exploring it. It is a sleepy, old, peaceful place, with the kind of traditional houses I love, and long-abandoned mercantile premises near the dock with advertising signs nailed on them from an earlier era. It is a deep, enclosed harbor, with a narrow entrance, surrounded by protecting hills. On the side opposite to where the United Church sits, people have clustered together near the shoreline, and every inch of space has been claimed and is

Rodney, Moreton's Harbour.

used. I saw an expensive fence strung along a big bare outcrop of rock, the posts held in place by stones. Also a boat such as I hadn't seen for twenty or more years, but which was in use in my childhood by some of the older fishermen: a small, keeled rodney with a sloping, triangular stern of the kind used in big skiffs, no longer than a dory, not big enough to hold an engine. The old men would row, scull, or sail boats of this type to the fishing grounds. Can there be more than half a dozen of them left on the island?

Having seen all this, I wanted more, so headed on a few kilometers to Tizzard's Harbour, which hadn't figured in any literature I had read but which turned out to be old and delightful too. These two communities are changing, but slowly; they are out too far on the headland to shake off their age. Chambers of commerce and development associations have not yet meddled with them. No trendy cleric has urged them to get with it. They are, to some extent, relics of a former time. There is no deliberate effort to keep the modern age at arm's length. But how far away Toronto seems! How fenced-in is Tizzard's Harbour!

May I bring up the subject of fences? I do so here because on my way back from Tizzard's Harbour I spotted an old-style gap made of removable longers, placed horizontally on rungs nailed between two spanned stakes at either side. The gap allowed access to a neglected meadow. But even here the longers on the fence itself had been replaced by wire. Longer- and picket-fences—the traditional fences of Newfoundland—are becoming rarities. So are stiles. But if you are a lover of old fences, you may find occasional scenes to please you in the northern extremities of the island. On the Burin Peninsula too. Be watchful.

You might wish to pop off on route 346 to Cobbs Arm, Too Good Arm, and Pikes Arm. I had to go to Too Good Arm to seek an explanation for the name. It is on a long, narrow arm of the sea, with smallish houses spread out along its side; it has a fishing station look. You're on headland here; don't expect to see big woods. A little white horse trotted out

Gap, near Tizzard's Harbour.

towards the road and had a long, close look at me as I was taking snaps of some graplins piled into curious shapes. That was good. It *is* good here. But too good?

The turnoff to Herring Neck is farther out on 340. This community had a lot in it that interested me. First I sought out the Orange Lodge, where William Coaker founded the Fishermen's Protective Union (FPU) in November, 1908, an organization that became enormously influential in Newfoundland politics and society. I did find the Lodge; the two big steeple-like structures that fronted the building in 1908 have been reduced in size and topped by odd protuberances resembling wigwams. Otherwise it is much the same as it was in Coaker's day, though I am told it is now hardly ever used. The lovely old Society of United Fishermen (SUF) hall, high on a hill in another part of the harbor and bearing a sign saying "Purity, Love, Fidelity," also shows signs of neglect. VCR machines and television have taken their toll on social life in communities like this. Herring Neck is a beautiful place, spread out around inlets of the sea, with very old houses, many well maintained. Some of these houses were hauled over the ice to their present locations from elsewhere in nearby arms. Herring Neck is thus a place where people want to live, a going concern. But what exactly makes it go? Not fishing!

In 1992 I found much to photograph, including tomcod drying in the sun in a way I hadn't seen before, hanging by their tails from nails on the side of an ochred shed, and the rotting hulk

Tomcod drying, Herring Neck.

of an early longliner, lying on her side, waiting for the axe.

But let's go on. Twillingate is well worth an extended visit. I found a street sign here called "Pride's Drung," which reflects the local awareness of history, since drung (meaning lane) is a very old English word that lingers yet in Newfoundland speech. Twillingate has geared itself for the tourist trade in quite a vigorous way. I had a good time hanging around here. As an opera buff, I meant to search out the burial place of Georgina Stirling, a prima donna at the turn of the century who called herself Marie Toulinguet; other pleasures prevented this. The Anchor Inn (884-2777) has been recommended to me, but I haven't stayed there.

Now, let me take you to the very tip of this peninsula, Crow Head, a cape that is not well known to Newfoundlanders but which has high, sheer, menacing cliffs and astonishing views. There is a parking lot near the lighthouse, and you may walk around near the cliff's edge. Not too near. Obey the warning signs. Tie your kiddies to the fence. I have never been one to fear heights, but these gave me pause. Sea Breeze municipal park is nearby; it offers camping, a playground for children, a beach, and an excellent situation. Don't miss Crow Head.

View from Crow Head.

Gander; The Straight Shore

Gander used to be called "The Crossroads of the World," because trans-Atlantic air traffic used its airport extensively for refuelling. In the 1950s the great American airlines Pan-Am and TWA, the Dutch KLM, BOAC, Icelandic Airways, SAS from Scandinavia, and other companies, maintained offices and staff there. But in time propeller aircraft gave way to the big jets, which could overfly Gander. The airport remains, however, the heart of the local economy, and the international terminal evokes the glories of past years. It has an impressive large mural depicting the history of flight, and various exhibits of a historical nature. The town is young, modern, more sophisticated than other places of comparable size, somewhat *Canadian* in outlook and appearance, equipped to handle tourists; it has good shopping and services. Its central location tends to make it a busy place. It is well situated for prospective salmon fishermen and canoeists. The Gander River, which flows through Glenwood 20-odd km west, is one of Newfoundland's great salmon rivers. Gander Lake, huge and little used for boating, is an obvious attraction; at its southern extremity, the Northwest Gander River will take canoeists into the wilderness. When I can't camp, or am driving through on business, I tend to overnight at the Albatross Motel on the TCH, which has a reasonable dining room and a certain ambience. It is a place I'm used to and enjoy, though it can be noisy. It is also jerrybuilt, and you might have to drag luggage a long way.

Just east of Gander along the TCH you will find a Commonwealth War Graves Commission Cemetery, a forcible reminder of Gander's role in the Second World War. Gander was a crucial link in the Atlantic Air Ferry, through which warplanes were shipped to Britain to oppose the German menace. It is surprising to learn how many fliers died in Newfoundland in the darkest days of the War. Nearby, south of the TCH on a sideroad not well marked, is a monument to yet another tragedy: the crash of a chartered Arrow Air DC-8 in the pre-dawn of December 12, 1985, killing 248 U.S. soldiers (three of them women) and eight crew members. The monument, a very moving one, is called "Silent Witnesses." The troops were returning to the U.S. after serving as international peacekeepers on the Sinai Peninsula.

From Gander, you may head north on route 330 on what is known locally as "The Loop." The tall white birches in the vicinity of Gander quickly give way to the more characteristic evergreens, which turn into low scrub by the time you get to the Straight Shore (between Musgrave Harbour and Wesleyville), and then to barrens. This is flat, open country, ideal for bikers, I would think. There is very little traffic. When I last drove over this road, I marvelled at the buttercups and wild irises growing near the roadside—as beautiful, really, as the poppies of France or the heather of Scotland. Wherever you may be in Newfoundland, use your Peterson *Field Guide to Wildflowers of Northeastern and North-central North America* (which I trust you brought with you) to spot flowers as you drive

"Silent Witnesses"

along. Get out of the car and consider them. You will see purple goodwithy; daisies everywhere; the quite lovely and delicate cotton-grass, also white, on the southern marshes; cattail; white and purple clover flowers; blue harebells; the yellow golden-rod, a little later in summer; pink wild roses; deep pink fireweed; thistles, and many other kinds. Look for butterflies too. There is a booklet by A. Glen Ryan called *Some Newfoundland Butterflies*, distributed free by the Parks Division, Department of Tourism and Culture (address on page 29).

To backtrack just a little. At the community of Gander Bay, instead of turning northeast to Carmanville you could cross the bridge over the estuary of the Gander River and head northwest for 10 kilometers or so over route 331, maybe as far as Victoria Cove. This is another low, exposed coast, where the road passes close to the great open expanse of Gander Bay. It is a logging region; and I found a big, messy sawmill to photograph. But what really caught my eye along here was the Gander Bay boat, which I had read a lot about but hadn't really examined. It is a slim, long, lightweight boat, elegantly designed, combining ideas from the canoe and the skiff, well adapted for the outboard. These of course are used by guides and others on the Gander River, and you will see them also upriver at Glenwood.

Gander Bay boat.

But let's go back to the bridge and pick up route 330. After passing through Carmanville, I took a dirt road to Aspen Cove and Ladle Cove. This is lobstering country, exposed, flat, the water shallow. Ladle Cove is a great open cove with no cliffs, and houses strung along the road near the rocky beach. It is more an indentation than a cove. The very long beach is an ideal spot for beachcombing, and if you are one of those who wishes to return to the mainland of Canada with a lobster-pot on top of his car, you might well find such a pot here in early August. (Though you must not take one and run. Fishermen know where their damaged pots are and in due course will find them and repair those that can be repaired. So ask for the owner of your chosen pot, and be prepared to pay for it.) But walking along beaches, poking under rocks with sticks, watching the sandpipers and gulls, paddling in the water, examining the debris from old ocean, fingering the kelp—all this, as already hinted, is an available delight which you should not pass up, whether or not you want a lobster-pot. Kelp, by the way, is not eaten by Newfoundlanders, but this doesn't mean *you* can't eat it if you know how to prepare it. Nova Scotians among you probably do want to eat it. For recipes, see *Kelp for Better Health and Vitality*, by Frank Wilson. Ladle Cove is a remote, intriguing community.

It was in the bush near Musgrave Harbour that Sir Frederick Banting, the co-discoverer of insulin, met his doom in a plane crash in 1941, while en route to England. You will find a new Banting Motel in Ragged Harbour (part of Musgrave Harbour), which has efficiency units that look out over the ocean (655-2443; $54 single, $60 double), and a little farther down the road Sir Frederick Banting Memorial Park, a municipal park set on a flat meadow with good facilities for picnickers and campers. (The one institution that should have been called after Banting was the old Banting Memorial Hospital in Gander; but when a new regional hospital was opened there in the 1960s, it was named after a local physician, Dr. James Paton.) There is a white sandy beach at the park—quite an excellent beach, in fact—together with a pond where children can frolic in safety. The local authorities have rescued the skeleton of Banting's plane from the site where it crashed and placed it on the side of the road leading into the park: a ghoulish touch. Provincial authorities allowed it to be removed from the crash site because pieces were being sawed off by souvenir hunters.

I should say in passing that while people in Ragged Harbour do not appear to want to retain the name of their community, it is really a very distinguished name. I earlier quoted from Norman Duncan's collection of short stories, *The Way of the Sea*, published in 1903 (but available in a reprint); this book was set mostly in a place called Ragged Harbour—an imaginary setting, of course, but he could have taken the hint from the real place, since it was of the northern coast of the island that he was writing. *The Way of the Sea* is one of the best books ever written about Newfoundland. Duncan was a Canadian.

I regret to say that certain of the old racy names of Newfoundland, such as Ragged Harbour, have been cast aside by residents anxious to acquire respectability. Thus Devil's Cove has become Job's Cove, Distress is now St. Bride's, Hibbs' Hole is now on the map as Hibbs' Cove, Cuckhold's Cove in Trinity Bay is Dunfield, Scilly Cove is Winterton, Famish Gut is Fairhaven, Gay Side is Baytona, etc. A name such as Duntara or Baytona or Summerville is sure to have been concocted by a modern renovator. Dildo and South Dildo, Trinity Bay, and Dildo Run in

Notre Dame Bay have unexpectedly survived this onslaught. But I fear for their future, as I do for that of Horney Head, Backside Pond, Harry's Knob, Pussey's Gully, The Nook, Hauling Cove, Skin Cabin Pond, Gin Cove, Ass Hill, Head Harbour, Honey Pot Island, Dyke Lake, Queer Island, Jigger Tickle, Fairy Island, Blowhole, Dick Rock, Ball Island, Little Coney Arm, Lousy Rock, Safe Harbour, Piss Pot Hill, Cuckhold Head, Hug My Dug Island, Cock Bank, and many more.

The road from Musgrave Harbour to Lumsden follows a flat, low coast, just about empty of trees and, on a clear day, offering striking views of land, sea, and offshore islands. After Lumsden, a clean, prim town, you may wish to pull off and enjoy the delights of Windmill Bight provincial park, where there is a splendid beach of white sand and a place to swim. Then go along the dirt sideroad to Cape Freels—I mean the cape itself rather than the nearby community of the same name. (Not that I have anything against *it*.) To get near the cape, simply do not turn left into the community; drive straight on. You will find yourself on a large sand flat which has trails mainly created by ATVs. Go as far as you think safe, then get out and walk. (If you go farther and get stuck in sand ruts or mud, don't blame me.) After about a couple of miles from the turnoff to the community, you will come to another big white beach—a glorious spot for bird-watching, sunning, hiking, or even driving golf balls! Thats how flat and big it is. In my four-wheel drive Chevy Blazer, I must confess that I followed a local pick-up all the way to the remote beach, but not without some harrowing moments. It was well worth the effort. The beach at Cape Freels is one of Newfoundland's finest places. In late July, 1991, I saw sooty shearwaters (hagdowns) there; they are normally offshore birds that came inshore on this occasion, I presume, for the caplin, which were late arriving all around the island. (However, there were no caplin on the beach the day I visited.)

Newtown and Wesleyville are old towns perched on fingers of rock sticking out in the ocean. They form a really remarkable sight, especially the latter; the people who live there must sense the closeness of the sea all the time, hear every lop and swish it makes. Not very far out to sea there are flat sunkers and islands where big, delicious mussels can be picked off the rocks. You just boil them for five minutes or so. A feast! A fisherman may take you out and show you where to get them, if he has time. Do not be afraid to approach fishermen to be taken out to offshore islands or to abandoned communities that are inaccessible by road. They are sometimes very willing to do this. You must be prepared to pay, of course; negotiate the amount before departure to avoid any subsequent misunderstanding. Going out in a fishing boat just to look around at the land and ocean is one of the most pleasurable experiences Newfoundland has to offer. Central Canadians may think it is the same as being on a lake; it is not the same. The surge of the great waves, the smell, the vast spaces, the salt spray in your face when there's a breeze, perchance a whale breaching and blowing nearby—these things are different. Whale-watching is now practised all around the island. Get one of these books: *Wet and Fat: Whales and Seals of Newfoundland and Labrador*, by John Lien, Leesa Fawcett, Sue Staniforth, drawings by Don Wright ($9.95); or *A Guide to the Photographic Identification of Whales based on their Natural and Acquired Markings*, by John Lien and Steven Katona ($6.95).

To come back to Newtown and Wesleyville. There is much local pride in these towns, and if truth be told there is much to take pride in. The architecture of older houses here, and of the churches, is highly pleasing; the Barbour house in Newtown is very impressive. Houses are generally well kept up. As stated earlier, many Newfoundlanders have discarded the saltbox and other house designs of their forefathers in their hurry to get into the three-bedroom bungalow, or worse; not so here. These are towns famous for sealing and seafaring.

Back on the TCH heading south towards Gambo,.a tiresome drive awaits you—unless you happen to be a sports fisherman. The Indian Bay area is one of the best parts of the island for trouting. Did you bring that canoe I suggested you buy? This is the place to make use of it. Check the map: there are many choice ponds to your right as you drive south. But note: Indian Bay Big Pond and Little Bear Cave Pond, both in the Indian Bay Brook watershed, are closed to trout fishing in 1994.

Eastport Peninsula;
Terra Nova National Park

I suppose you can call it a peninsula, but it is a very small one. As you come south on the TCH, the best way to get to it is to turn off on 310, through Glovertown and Traytown, towns whose economies are centered on Terra Nova National Park, and which are well set up for the tourist trade. This peninsula is one of the places on the island that has been "developed for tourism": you'll find private camping grounds, cabins, an inn, a "family funland," and such things, in Eastport itself, not too far from the beach. I daresay children would like it around here. The beach is of white sand and is not very long or wide, but it seems to be a favorite spot for vacationers. There are a few picnic tables near the sand, and changing rooms for those wishing to sun or attempt to swim, but no fresh water. Do not spurn the little beach: Newfoundland, as hinted earlier, has far too much rock, and not enough sand. So when you see a sandy beach, lie on it and let your children dig in it. The outports in the general area of Eastport, Burnside (from which the ferry leaves for St.

Brendan's), St. Chads, Happy Adventure, and others, are charming in a somewhat Nova Scotian way. Salvage is exquisite: go and have a look.

Back on the TCH and halfway through Terra Nova National Park, you will find route 301, a dirt road about 20 km long to the community of Terra Nova. This is a sort of gateway to the eastern Newfoundland wilderness. A wilderness tour company in fact operates out of the town, and it is well placed for canoeists, as a glance at the map will show. It is an isolated, well cared for, quiet, appealing little town, with a different look and feel to it from places of comparable size on the ocean. I think artists might like it.

Terra Nova National Park is 400 square kilometers in size. Its main theme is "boreal landscapes touching sheltered seas," boreal being a term describing a geographic region of mainly coniferous forests. Forests, ponds, and ocean are mainly what this park has to offer. Or, to quote the Superintendent's own description, the Park comprises "gently undulating granite hills, cradling [!] a host of lakes, ponds, and bogs; a boreal forest with its shoreline lapped [!] by the cold Atlantic Ocean and Labrador Current; a deeply indented coastline, graced with magnificent [!] seastacks, caves and arches; and a diversity of birds and mammals." As my square brackets will suggest, I think this a trifle overstated: compared with Gros Morne, Terra Nova is dull. On a recent May 24 long weekend, the authorities decided to prohibit drinking within the Park, which made it even duller and reduced the population considerably. A note of high seriousness is sounded in the Park's literature. Thus visitors are "challenged" to keep "this special place free of pollution" and to "continue those practices in your homes and communities." A "Green Committee" meets regularly to monitor activities and "Green messages are posted regularly." And so on.

The last time I visited I was put off by all this ponderousness, having quite enough of it in my normal place of work, and went south to Thorburn Lake Provincial Park, where I swam in the cold deep lake and reflected on the sea-planes taking off and landing a few hundred yards away: a highly peculiar business to be going on in a park.

I fear I have been unfair to Terra Nova park. People go there, spend their entire vacation, and return year after year for more. I have myself had very happy times there. It is well regulated, well serviced, and as varied as such a setting can be. You can camp year-round, go on "ocean tours," swim at Sandy Pond, hike to remote sites or the top of a "mountain," fish, golf at the Twin Rivers Golf Course (see "Other Sports," above), watch beavers working, go canoeing, rent mountain bikes or kayaks from concessionaires, go on long walks with an interpreter, etc. For information, write: Terra Nova National Park, Glovertown, Nfld. A0G 2L0 (phone 533-2801).

The Discovery Trail

This is the name given to route 230 and its offshoots on the Bonavista Peninsula (watch for a turnoff about 12 km before Clarenville, a way to avoid much slow traffic). It is a well-forested area, by Newfoundland standards, with a goodly bit of agriculture as well as fishing. You will see stalls for vegetables; and, farther out, be able to buy lobster from fishermen, for this is a great lobstering region. The big towns are Bonavista, Catalina, and Trinity (of which, more later); but Port Union, center of the old FPU, already alluded to, should not be neglected. When you get there, ask the whereabouts of the monument to Coaker, the FPU's founder. You will note that, strangely, he has his broad back to the ocean; he glowers inland, over a barren, as if in despair of the sea ever offering fishermen anything but misery. The FPU motto, *suum cuique*, "to each his own," has always struck me as a peculiar one for a collectivist enterprise. Look for Coaker's house as well, plus a museum with a lot in it about the FPU.

But I'm getting ahead of myself. As you head northeast from Clarenville on 230, you can shoot off to the small communities around Goose Bay or Sweet Bay. Take 235, drive through Summerville to the end of settlement, and walk out on the headland: a gorgeous cove awaits you, a beach, and forlorn graveyard. Before getting to King's Cove, turn off just past Plate Cove East to Open Hall, Red Cliff, and Tickle Cove. Observe Tickle Cove Pond, the setting of a ballad describing the rescue of a mare named Kit from drowning, recently sung well by Ron Hynes on the CD "Another Time." The road stops at Tickle Cove, but if you go to the very end of it you will see that a footpath carries on beyond the Anglican and Methodist cemeteries along shore. I have walked far on this path—almost, I think, to Keels. The landscape is strange, with great finger-like, red rocks pointing out to sea as if to say, Look there! But there is nothing out there. Not on the days I looked, anyway. Let me pause to say there are often terrific walks at the end of highroads in Newfoundland, as the road dwindles to the ancient cart tracks of the early settlers, and then to footpaths, now little used. There are similar paths at Keels and King's Cove. That at Keels takes you to the pond where the locals swim, but before you get to it you can see in the

Author beachcombing, near Keels.

rocks the devil's footprints; if you go on beyond the pond and over a hill you come to a cove filled with driftwood, a great place for picking cranberries or just hanging out to poke around in the debris. When you park your car near the wharf in King's Cove, you will see a good path stretching off towards the lighthouse. Some local people take vehicles out there, but I wouldn't recommend it. It is, however, a splendid short walk, which ends at the lighthouse with a commanding view of Blackhead Bay and of Cape Bonavista in the distance. (Interested in lighthouses? Get *Lighthouses of Newfoundland and*

Autumn Path, King's Cove.

Labrador, by David John Molloy, $24.95.) At Lady's Cove on this path picnic tables have been placed on the cliff edge, and steps have been built down to the cove itself.

I don't want to skip too quickly over Keels and King's Cove. The former is likely to be spoiled soon by a slate quarry , but it has been until lately such an isolated place that many of the old houses are preserved, perched out on rocks in quite a jaunty way. King's Cove, a community known, and rightly known, for the learning of its early inhabitants, is the ancestral home of the Devines, one of the island's most distinguished literary families. P.K. Devine's *In the Good Old Days!* has been published recently, patched together from Devine's newspaper articles about life in King's Cove in the late 19th and early 20th centuries. Excellent reading. The old-style houses at King's Cove are worth studying; alas, some are in decay. Note the Roman Catholic Church, looking out over a part of the community that is now totally deserted. Once on the sea's edge, King's Cove has crept back from the headland to the

Lighthouse, King's Cove.

cosy harbor, and beyond that to the sheltering hills. As in many other places, the older houses are near the sea; back toward and along the main road are the up-to-date residences of teachers and other professionals.

Go along 235 through Stock Cove and Knights Cove and Amherst Cove—a coastline on which, when there are northerly winds, the waves pile up magnificently. The road stays close to water, and there are places to picnic and walk and stare at the great ocean. This lonely shore is one of my favorite places.

Bonavista, a town that has more one-way streets than Belfast, is a big service center for the peninsula, with a hospital, government offices, and shops. It is spread out on a bleak flat headland of rock, empty of vegetation as such headlands almost always are. Though it is slightly mocked in the ballad "I'se the B'y,"

> I don't want your maggoty fish,
> That's no good for winter;
> I can buy as good as that,
> Down in Bonavista,

it is in fact a busy and important place. The cape itself is the alleged landfall of John Cabot in 1497, though the wording on the official plaque at the site does not affirm such. Nor should it. The truth is that nobody knows where Cabot sighted land on his voyage from Bristol. It might well have been here; but could have been somewhere else, maybe even (dread thought!) Cape Breton. But there is much talk and to-do about Cabot as 1997 approaches. Cape Bonavista, with its great cliffs and stark, rocky, grim scenery, plus the squat red and white reconstructed lighthouse, is not to be missed, whatever you believe about Cabot. A place to stay in Bonavista? Try Hotel Bonavista, 2 km outside of town on 230 (468-1510; $52 single, $5 extra per person). This is not a lounge; it's a well-kept, modern hotel.

On your way back from Bonavista, you might pop off to Elliston, formerly Bird Island Cove, which I happen to have a strong interest in because one of the earliest Newfoundland-born writers, Philip Tocque, already mentioned, kept a pedlar's shop there and wrote a queer book called *Wandering Thoughts or Solitary Hours*. Tocque was an enthusiast for Newfoundland, and promoted its tourist potential to outsiders in such sentences as: "Nought is heard to disturb the solitude save now and then the notes of the ptarmigan"; and "Sunstrokes are entirely unknown." But Tocque or no

At Elliston.

Tocque, Elliston is an appealing place, with a number of quite exquisite older houses. Be sure to walk out on Elliston Point, from which both Bird Islands are visible, though a little further down towards Maberly (pronounced mab, not mabe) there is a provincial park (a lookout site only) which offers the birdwatcher a closer view of the more southerly one. At Sandy Cove, between Elliston and Maberly, there is a beach with a playground: a good place for children to knock around. The isolated outport of Maberly is striking. If you are in the mood for a walk, find your way to a path south of the community—you can drive on it for a few hundred meters—and then head over the barrens along the cliffs. The cliffs are high, so keep your distance. This is a stunning, open terrain, and if you want a long walk, you could without much trouble find your way to Little Catalina along a shoreline empty of human life.

Maberly.

Port Rexton and Trinity East, south on 230, are gorgeous old communities, access to which is gained by leaving the main road and poking around on streets and lanes. At Trinity East, you might stay at Peace Cove Inn (464-3738/3419; off-season 781-2255; $41, $45, $48), an old house tastefully renovated. The owner, Art Andrews, also conducts boat tours. Trinity itself has geared up for tourism in a big way. A Trinity Loop Fun Park has assorted attractions, a train even! Hiscock House shows you how the other half used to live. You can easily find someone to take you out on a boat whale-watching, an activity that most people like and that appears to be a specialty of Trinity, though you can watch whales anywhere in Newfoundland. The last time I did so was in Pouch Cove harbor, just north of St. John's, in August; a half dozen immense humpbacks decided to hang around there for about two weeks chasing caplin, perhaps aware that a swarm of irate federal officials would descend on anyone who interfered with them. (By the way, pronounce pouch in Pouch Cove as if it were a dog.) Trinity is one of two towns in Newfoundland that remind me of towns in New England: the other is Brigus. The streets and houses in both places speak of regularity, money, cultivation. People of means lived here, and apparently still do.

Proceed to Trouty and New Bonaventure. There ask directions to Kearley's Harbour, which is not on the map because it is a "resettled community," i.e., nobody lives there any more. But there is a well-trodden path to it, about 2 km in length. Do take the path. Kearley's Harbour is a beautiful place, so much so that you wonder why people left it in the first place and why others haven't moved back. It seems a perfect spot for fishing, with naturally formed wharf-like rocks and deep water in close. If you really want an adventure, backpack down to British Harbour, further south. This will get you into rough terrain. Not for those with weak ankles or faint hearts.

The Burin Peninsula

At Goobies on the TCH, turn off on route 210 to the Burin Peninsula, a long southern leg-like extension of the island. It has good roads and five substantial towns: Marystown, Burin, St. Lawrence, Fortune, and Grand Bank. These tend to share services on a regional basis, but each has its own special claim to fame; all are worth visiting and exploring. Marystown, the largest center, has a shipyard that notoriously has tottered on the edge of bankruptcy for decades but still manages to function, though not without help from the taxpayer. Fishery Products International (FPI), which in 1991 added a protein-processing unit to its fishplant in Marystown, is a big player in the economy, as it is in Burin and Fortune. There is no part of Newfoundland more dependent on fish than this peninsula; as a consequence, the future looks bleak.

Fortune is also the gateway to the French islands of St. Pierre and Miquelon. (Call SPM Tours at 722-3892 for reservations and information; the *Arethusa* has daily crossings from Fortune from mid-June to mid-September. Or call Lake & Lake Ltd. in Burin, 832-1950, which operates the *St. Eugene*.) St. Lawrence is a mining town, or rather *was* a mining town, for the fluorspar mine on which its economy was built has shut down, apparently for good. Grand Bank is famous in Newfoundland as the center of the old schooner fishery on the Grand Banks, which flourished between the 1880s and 1940s—decades when there still were fish on the Grand Banks. Its FPI plant closed in 1991. Marystown, Burin, and Fortune have a somewhat more modern, bustling look. Things are still a-building, the hum of commerce can be heard. The other two places are more subdued, more inclined to the backward glance. There is a miners' museum at St. Lawrence and a fishermen's museum at Grand Bank. Both places have a keen sense of history. As mines and fishplants close, that might well be all they are left with. Fortune excepted, the future probably belongs to the Placentia Bay side of the peninsula, the side which, I confess, I have always preferred.

You will have little trouble finding accommodations in the five towns, should you not wish to camp in one of the provincial parks. On business trips, I tend to stay at the Motel Mortier, Marystown (279-1600; $45, $62, $73 plus tax, depending on the part of the hotel you choose). This will not be to everybody's taste, but I'm used to it. Marystown is the biggest of the towns, and its location is such that you can make it a base for exploring the southern and more populous half of the peninsula. If you want to stay in the northern part of the peninsula, you might try the Kilmory Resort in Swift Current (549-2410/2204; large cabins holding up to six, $85 per day in season, $5 extra per person, children under 12 free.)

Back to 210. Beyond Swift Current, a beautiful open harbor on a long ocean sound, the road ascends to high, bare, plateau-like terrain, with wide expanses of bog, barrens, ponds, and low trees:

O rugged land!
Land of the rock and moss!
Land whose drear barrens it is woe to cross!
Thou rough thing from God's hand!

as the poet Lowell said. I have rarely driven over this region without the accompaniment of fog and rain—perhaps I have just been unlucky. Those who come from afar will doubtless find things to admire in the gullies, hills, and mists, but I sometimes have to ask, with the rustic character in one of Hardy's novels, "What are picturesque ravines and mists to us who see nothing else?" It is a long and tiresome ride down the rocky spine of this peninsula.

My last time down, I turned southeast along the new but poor dirt road to Monkstown on Paradise Sound. (There are quite a few places on the island with the name of Paradise.) This is a road of some 25 km, and I wouldn't advise trying it unless your tires are good. It is not much used; on a Sunday afternoon in fall, I passed one car on my way to Monkstown, two on my way back. There are opportunities along this road for fishing and canoeing, as indeed there are along 210 itself. Why go down to Monkstown? It is a remote outharbor, on a deep, sheltered sound that leads (should you want to go boating) to long-abandoned Darby Harbour and the living communities of South East Bight and Petit Forte. And it survived! The Smallwood government's "resettlement" scheme of the 1950s and '60s destroyed most of the remote places in Placentia Bay. These people for some reason resisted it, though how long they will continue to stay now that the road has been put through remains a question. There can't be more than fifty residents here. It looks rudimentary, rough, tentative, light years away from the glitter of Marystown even, let alone St. John's; hardly a place, it would seem, to keep the dictatorial Smallwood from getting his way. Far prettier spots than this have yielded to the alders and birches. Yet hold out it did. A government wharf is seen, but what government built it? Perhaps the Commission of Government in the 1930s. That's how antique it looks. A few splendid old houses suggest the past glories of Monkstown, if glories there ever were. There is an elementary school. What hermitic type teaches in it?

Speaking of hermits, I have a feeling that the remote islands and out-of-the-way shoreline indentations of Placentia Bay harbor a number of them. I met one such man at Davis Cove, a summer fishing station near Monkstown where I went to try to get a view of Merasheen Island. The fog prevented that. But I did meet and talk at length with this 58-year-old recusant, whose name and place of residence I will not divulge, although he was eager to divulge them to me. He lived alone, he said, because he didn't want to be intruded upon by policemen and bureaucrats and politicians. He had a whole community to himself; his house had two television sets, a telephone, and a radio of course, so that Cowper's imagined complaint of the marooned sailor Alexander Selkirk,

I am out of humanity's reach,
I must finish my journey alone,
Never hear the sweet music of speech,
I start at the sound of my own,

does not apply to him. "Three's Company" comes to him as quickly as it does to the citizens of Monkstown. He also has two fiberglass boats, hot and cold running water, propane gas heating, and other amenities. He keeps a supply of penicillin on hand over the winter, together with aspirin and other medicines. Guess what? He seems to be a happy man.

Just along 210 after the Monkstown turnoff is the road to Terrenceville, from which a Marine Atlantic ferry makes three departures per week in summer for ports to Burgeo, intersecting with a similar ferry heading from Port aux Basques to Hermitage. (For information—no reservations are accepted—phone 695-7081/7082; 1993 fare from Terrenceville to Port aux Basques, $49.70). The ferries are approximately 90 feet in length; they move fast, they have no cabins, and they call at the following ports: Rencontre East, English Harbour West, Harbour Breton, Hermitage, Gaultois, McCallum, Francois, Grey River, Ramea, Burgeo, Grand Bruit (pronounced brit), La Poile, and Port aux Basques. A glance at the map will show you that eight of these communities have no road connection to other communities. So if you take this ferry route, you can stop off at truly remote outports, ones that may never be hooked up to the highway system of the island.

Having gone to Monkstown and Davis Cove for a taste of the primitive, you may want, a little further on, to turn down to Boat Harbour and Brookside for the scenic route, for these are quite lovely places, the most picturesque along this coast. The road from Brookside to remote Petit Forte was completed in 1992. Do go and see this legendary place which, like Monkstown, refused to give in to the blandishments of Smallwood. Parker's Cove, a more compact, rougher-looking spot, and Baine Harbour are old communities in the process of modernizing. The latter is situated on a long arm of Placentia Bay; very inviting. As in northern Newfoundland, many fishermen along this coast maintain their own premises—a sign of independence, of course, and of respect for tradition. The lobster fishery in these parts has evidently been a success. There is evidence of prosperity. One fisherman in Baine Harbour has christened his fish-house "Ocean Bride." Mind you, he could be using irony.

Premises, Baine Harbour.

You will want to turn off to Jean de Baie, if only because of the intriguing name. It is very thinly populated; houses are spread out along a saltwater pond, and on the ocean there is a sandy beach—a dirty, kelpy beach when I last looked at it, but one where the enterprising traveller will find room to lie around and get a suntan, supposing the sun comes out to do the tanning. The channel between pond and ocean lets in and out the tide in a fashion which, in New Brunswick, would lead it to be termed a "reversing falls" or some such notable thing.

It is hard to look at some of these Placentia Bay outports and not be tempted by the seclusion they offer.

Beyond Marystown, find your way to 220, the road around the boot. Stop at St. Lawrence; stay a while. There is much to see and do here. On my last visit, having reread Cassie Brown's book *Standing into Danger*, I determined to find my way to the cliff-top monument commemorating the *Truxtun* and *Pollux* disaster. It was of course the cliff and site I really wanted to see. The plaque itself is not all that impressive. (There are other commemorative plaques in St. Augustus Cemetery and the Community Health Centre, which is what the hospital given to the people by the American government is now called; a sculpted monument called Echoes of Valour is in front of the Town Hall.)

The *Truxtun* and *Pollux* were two of three U.S. destroyers which came ashore in a storm in the early morning of February 18, 1942, within a few miles of one another on the coast between St. Lawrence and Lawn, with a loss of 203 lives. Thus it was a tragedy of major proportions, although it could have been worse: 185 sailors were rescued, and in the rescue the people of Lawn and St. Lawrence, as Cassie Brown shows, played heroic roles. One of the ships, the *Truxtun*, ran aground in Chambers Cove, close to St. Lawrence. That is where the monument is.

To get there, you must drive through St. Lawrence and find your way to the lousy dirt road that leads past the old mine site. Sometimes there are markers along the way, but you can't count on them being there. Mischief-makers pull them down. There is a big fork in the road after a couple of kilometers: keep to the right. Cross a bridge, and you will see at once a couple of tracks leading to the right. Do not take those. Instead, park your vehicle, and begin walking on the well-worn footpath to the left. That is the path to the monument. You have a stiff walk ahead of you—about 20 minutes—but it is pleasant enough on a clear day. Soon you break out of the trees and come to Chambers Cove itself, a pastoral, lonely spot, ideal for picnicking; camping too, perhaps, though campers will be disturbed by those looking for the monument and by ATVs. Look past

Cliffs where the Truxton came ashore..

Chambers Cove to the hill above it and you will see towards the right a big wooden cross. That stands above the monument.

The climb up to the monument is along a grassy footpath. You are now on top of the high cliffs over which the oil-soaked sailors of the *Truxtun* who managed to get ashore were hauled. Do not get too close! The ground tends to give away near the edge. It is a forbidding and melancholy scene.

The bodies of the sailors who were buried in St. Lawrence were later disinterred and taken back to the U.S. I am told that one American remains buried in Lamaline.

Towards Lamaline we must now go. After leaving St. Lawrence, you find yourself driving through great, flat, mostly treeless, open, empty areas of bog, virtually at sea level, with flattish islands visible offshore. This is the typical low wetland of the Burin Peninsula's boot. From Lawn westward, communities such as Lord's Cove, Taylor's Bay, and Lamaline itself have a look unlike that of most Newfoundland outports: because there is plenty of flat bog to build on, houses are spread out in a sprawling way somewhat reminiscent of prairie farming communities. This exposed and muddy region has apparently not prospered of late. Maybe peat-cutting has a future. Anything connected with bog should work! As well, the proximity of St. Pierre (about 11 km from Point May) no doubt has benefited those willing to take a few risks on foggy nights.

At Lamaline, I found my way to Allan's Island, the southernmost tip of the peninsula, connected by causeway to the mainland, and had a relaxed look at land and sea. There is a passage in Hardy where he exclaims against conventional notions of charm and beauty. "The time seems near," he wrote, "when the chastened sublimity of a moor or sea will be all of nature that is absolutely in keeping with the moods of the more thinking among mankind; and ultimately, to the commonest tourist, spots like Iceland may become what the vineyards and myrtle-gardens of southern Europe are to him now, and Heidelberg and Baden be passed unheeded as he hastens from the Alps to the sand-dunes of Scheveningen."

Or to the mud-flats of Lamaline. Foggy though it often is, the boot of Burin will have its day in the sun.

Isthmus of Avalon; Trinity Bay; Conception Bay to Harbour Grace

The Avalon Peninsula is the part of Newfoundland first settled permanently by Europeans, and hence is often said to be the most "historic" part of the island. As already suggested, this is a Eurocentric and mildly racist view. Yet to be fair, there is a goodly bit of history to be savored here. And more than history. While it is densely populated by local standards, especially the northeast corner and the western side of Conception Bay, the peninsula still has plenty of wilderness and wildlife and long stretches of lonely highways. As on the west coast of the island, there is enough to see and do in this area to consume your entire vacation. If you want to go directly to the Avalon, skipping the rest of Newfoundland, you can take the Marine Atlantic ferry from North Sydney to Argentia in Placentia Bay. This service operates twice-weekly from mid-June until the end of September: the ferry leaves North Sydney on Tuesday, returning Wednesday; and leaves North Sydney again on Friday, returning Saturday. North Sydney departure time: 7:00 a.m.; Argentia departure time: 9:00 a.m. (This is the 1994 pattern, as described to me in February. Changes are possible; you might check with the Marine Atlantic Office in St. John's, 772-5700, to confirm it.)

The narrow isthmus of Avalon commences at Come By Chance in Placentia Bay and runs between that bay on the south and west and Trinity Bay to the north and east. At times, on certain high elevations along the road through the isthmus—not always, because fog is common here—you can see both bays at once: Trinity, which until recently was a peaceful, rural retreat, far removed from modern industrial experiment; and Placentia, a magnificent wide bay, already besmirched with the spills and fumes that are associated with an oil refinery. You see the refinery spewing its flame and smog as you pass Come By Chance, a high pollutant industry in a pastoral setting—perhaps a sign of what the future holds for this island. You smell it too, if the wind is right. A vile smell it is! The only possible reason for building a refinery in this spot (it was officially opened in 1973, long before the discovery of oil at Hibernia, then mothballed, then opened again) was that inhabitants of the market area in the eastern U.S. didn't want its stench near their homes, but didn't mind it being near ours. Who can blame them? Many beaches of Placentia Bay are, as you might expect, contaminated with oily debris from the tankers that bring the crude to the refinery and take the refined products away; hence numerous seabirds are killed each year. Who knows how many? We see only the ones that drift onto certain beaches. Again, who knows what is happening to the fish? The only good thing that has occurred in Placentia Bay in many a year has been the closing of the ERCO phosphorous plant at Long Harbour, another odious polluter of the environment. Like the refinery, this was brought to Newfoundland by J.R. Smallwood, who offered big hydro subsidies to get it here. It was so vile that a 1977 study reported that for a distance of 5 km northeast of the plant over 80% of spruce and fir trees had been killed by fluoride emissions. You can guess what the effects were on animals within the same radius.

A new "industry" is now being discussed: freighting domestic garbage from the eastern seabord of the U.S. to be burnt at Long Harbour. See how fast we learn in these parts?

Now, at last, Trinity Bay is to get its share of development, for at Great Mosquito Cove on the isthmus the Gravity Based Structure (GBS) and one of the five topside modules for the Hibernia offshore oil project are being built. The GBS is a massive concrete object, to be perched on the Grand Banks southeast of St. John's, on which modules of bewildering complexity will sit for distribution of Hibernia "sweet crude" to tankers. After Hibernia dries up, the GBS will probably stay where it is in the north Atlantic—a man-made island. You can't just leave the TCH to have a look at what is happening at Great Mosquito Cove. Security guards will stop you. But an information center has been constructed at the turnoff to Mosquito Cove, from which guided tours of the site are conducted every day in summer, commencing at 2:00 p.m. The bus holds 48; first come, first served. Phone 463-6306 for information. Mosquito Cove is one of the biggest construction projects in the history of Canada.

Don't just drive by communities like Arnold's Cove, Southern Harbour, Little Harbour, and Fair Haven in Placentia Bay, and Sunnyside, Chance Cove, Norman's Cove, and Chapel Arm in Trinity Bay. A detour from the TCH to explore one or more of these places is a good idea. Arnold's Cove was one of the "growth centers" to which people from the islands and smaller communities around Placentia Bay were moved in J.R. Smallwood's resettlement scheme, already alluded to—another of his brilliant ideas, to add to those noted.

At Whitbourne, I suggest turning off on route 80 and spinning through the rather lovely eastern side of Trinity Bay, whose gently sloping landscapes and low cliffs always remind me of parts of New England. At South Dildo you will see whalebone gateposts on the roadside, a reminder that whaling was once a big industry in the area. Carino Co. Ltd. of this town is a processor of seal pelts. Thanks to animal rights activists and Ottawa's lack of backbone, whaling and sealing, once vital to the Newfoundland economy, now contribute little or nothing to it. (There is a whaling and sealing museum in South Dildo.) The old town of New Harbour is the birthplace of the writer Ron Pollett, a humorist whose nostalgic sketches appeared in the 1940s and '50s but who didn't make a noise on the mainland; had he done so, there'd be a monument

Gateposts, South Dildo.

to him here. A little past New Harbour, you come to Fish-out Pond, part of a fish hatchery where you can catch your own rainbow trout. (Gear may be rented; you pay by the pound for what you catch.) Whiteway has a Women's Institute Craft Shop of which I have heard much praise. Heart's Delight and Heart's Desire surely can't be resisted! Heart's Content, a fair-sized, picturesque town, is also worth stopping at. Here the first trans-Atlantic cable was landed in July, 1866, a big event in the story of communications, which you can investigate in the local museum. The cable station in Heart's Content closed in the 1960s.

Go on to Old Perlican and east along route 70 to Bay de Verde, Conception Bay, one of my favorite places, before 1992 a real fishing community, the harbor clogged with boats, the wharf in summer humming with activity, with boys selling cod-tongues, men cleaning fish, etc. Bay de Verde smelled of fish then—the way a Newfoundland outport should smell.

Flambro' Head, on your way south on 70, is a great spot to birdwatch; the cliffs here are high and very dangerous. It is a haunted Head, so camping on it is not recommended.

At Burnt Point, O'Flaherty's Grocery is a good place to buy groceries and supplies. Northern Bay, a mile or so further, has the best beach I have seen in Newfoundland, a beach of gorgeous, fine, dark, basaltic sand. Northern Bay Sands provincial park offers well-positioned campsites and picnic sites in a lovely setting. You are getting close to St. John's, so summer weekends attract big crowds; avoid weekends, and

Northern Bay Sands.

the beach is practically deserted. Hogan's Cabins (584-3380/3851; $50 double, plus taxes) are conveniently located near the beach. (Another fine beach is further along the shore at Salmon Cove.)

Western Bay has a monument to its most famous son, the poet E.J. Pratt, who left Newfoundland for Canada when he was 25, but the Methodist manse he was born in was not located where the monument is; you have to go off the road towards the vacated community of Bradley's Cove. After a few hundred meters you will see a cemetery on your right, and the manse used to be across the road from it. Note Western Bay Point farther out on the road: a good place for a hike. As is Bradley's Cove, to which you may drive. A few foundations of root cellars, broken fences, and broken rock walls are what remains at the spot where Bradley's Cove once was.

Speaking of cellars and walls, you will see not a few of these artifacts along this shore, a rocky, wild, high coastline that made great demands of settlers. (In some places, fish had to be hoisted to the bank with booms and trolleys.) Owing to the hard winters, the walls here do not last as long as they do in Ireland, so that what you have left now are piles of rock rather than orderly arrangements. Some venerable walls, for instance the one that used to be in front of the old Roman Catholic church in Western Bay, have been broken up by renovating pastors. Cellars, which thirty or forty years ago were vital protectors of vegetables against frost, are also mostly in ruins; the flat stones of which their sides were constructed have been removed to make wells or walkways. The best cellars I have seen in Newfoundland are at Keels and Maberly, Bonavista Bay.

As you head further south on 70, you will pass near two more resettled communities: Gusset's Cove and Spout Cove. Gusset's Cove

Abandoned cellars, near Maberly.

(across the road and down a lane from Blackhead United Church) was an Irish settlement. Only the graveyard remains. Wander down to the salt water, sit on the rocks, and eat your sandwich or apple. A gorgeous setting. Spout Cove (just past the fine old community of Kingston, on the left) has been immortalized in a local song, "Where Spout Cove Used To Be," written by Leo King. I don't want to leave the North Shore (as the coast between Salmon Cove and Bay de Verde is known; a few years ago somebody from a place adjacent to Carbonear wrote a memoir called *From the Nart' Shore*, not realizing he wasn't from the North Shore at all!)—I say, I don't want to leave the shore without noting that Blackhead is the site of the first Methodist church to be built in what is now Canada. It was built in the winter of 1768-9, by the congregation of the Irish-speaking missionary Laurence Coughlan, who was sent by John Wesley to Newfoundland, probably to convert Roman Catholics. Instead, he mostly converted Anglicans.

On to Carbonear and Harbour Grace, old towns that were once the hub of trading and fishing in Conception Bay, and which today continue to play important roles in the commercial life of the region. They compete vigorously for whatever is going: thus Carbonear, which seems to be winning the competition so far, got the regional hospital; but the citizens of Harbour Grace have been promised a federal prison. And may even get it. (Why they would want it is another question.) But Harbour Grace has been codded by promises before this. In 1978-9 the people there were convinced their community would become a "super-port," a vital component in an elaborate fisheries scheme proposed by a cabinet minister of limited intellectual capacity but sound political instincts. It had something to do with collecting fish from all over the island, freezing it, and then—well, the diagram of the facility passed out by the aforesaid minister featured two smokestacks, so maybe the intention was to smoke it too. He announced all this in a slick and hilarious government pamphlet called *Fish is the Future*, now a collector's item, which was sent to every household in the province. Once free, these pamphlets are fetching $20; many fishermen can't afford them! At all events, the proposed "Development Program for the Fishing Industry," including the super-port, came to nothing, though the minister did well in the next election. And in subsequent ones. As I write this, he is still ensconced in the provincial cabinet, issuing "consultative documents" on the fishery. His latest was called *Changing Tides*, in which he projects "1997 landings" of Newfoundland groundfish (now virtually wiped out by draggers) at 250,000 tonnes!

But to return. The old parts of both Carbonear and Harbour Grace—mostly on Water Street in both towns, though Harvey Street in Harbour Grace has its attractions—are well worth exploring. Unfortunately, a lot of the older shops have lost out to the ugly Trinity-Conception Mall. Progress!

Carbonear Island held out against the enterprising Quebec raider Pierre Le Moyne d'Iberville in 1697; legend has it that the first French invader who stepped on land there was cloven in two by a burly Newfoundland swordsman. To mention one other famous person associated with this area: Amelia Earhart took off from the airport in Harbour Grace in 1932, thereby becoming the first woman to fly solo across the Atlantic.

I have had some pleasant stays at the Harbour Castle Inn, Water St., Harbour Grace (596-5156; $63 double, including GST; decent dining room). Outlying places such as Bristol's Hope, Freshwater, and Blow Me Down are venerable and worth a visit. Riverhead too.

Remember what I said earlier about Henry Winton. Find Saddle Hill; spare a thought for old Harry.

Towards St. John's

The road south of Harbour Grace to Holyrood, then northeast towards St. John's, passes through an assortment of towns that are looking more and more like a grubby suburbia as the years pass, though there are occasionally structures and scenes that demand a second look. To get a taste of what is left of old Newfoundland in the area, you have to get off the Conception Bay Highway to the smaller, tucked away places. Artists have been attracted to the outlying headland communities in this part of Conception Bay since the 19th century, one of the earliest being the Englishman William Gosse (brother of Philip Henry), who painted Ship

Cove on the Port de Grave "peninsula" in the 1840s. This narrow neck of land stretching out into the bay is something a visitor should see. It ends at Hibb's Cove, where there is a Fishermen's Museum, plus a building that, to its credit, clings to the name "Hibb's Hole School." This finger of rock also contains the fine old towns of Bareneed and Port de Grave. The sights out here are startling: bald rock, striking seascapes everywhere you turn, Bell Island and Cupids on one side, Bay Roberts on the other, old houses and sheds. Find your way back through Bareneed to Clarke's Beach; you will pass by one of the finest clusters of restored old homes to be seen anywhere on the Avalon.

Drive on to Cupids and Brigus (turning left off route 70 after South River). Cupids, as stated earlier, is the site of the first formal English colony in Newfoundland, and you will find a couple of monuments commemorating this fact. At one of these, there is what is said to be the biggest flagpole in the British Commonwealth, with the biggest Union Jack flying on it. You may think this of interest. Cupids is also the place where, in 1820, two British surrogate judges, one an Anglican priest, sentenced the Irish Catholic fisherman and epileptic James Landrigan to be whipped with the cat-o'-nine-tails for non-payment of a small debt to a merchant. His land was seized and sold to pay the debt. The whipping brought on an epileptic seizure and, eventually, a public furor that helped in the fight for self-government. Before long, he got his land back, and I understand it remains in the possession of his descendants. I didn't see a monument to Landrigan at Cupids.

I have already compared Brigus to Trinity, but for charm and, well, prettiness, Brigus has the edge. Friends of mine stop off at a tea room here; very jolly. The community has been well represented in art. A.E. Harris, an English emigrant, spent much of his three last years (1930-33) in Brigus and produced striking work. The great American artist Rockwell Kent lived here in 1914-15 but was forced to leave when inhabitants thought him a German spy. Brigus was once a humming center of the sealing and fishing industries. The most celebrated native son was Captain Bob Bartlett, who travelled to the Arctic with Robert Peary on his expeditions of 1905-6 and 1908-9. Bartlett went off to the U.S. to live, and in 1928 wrote a memoir lamenting the changes he'd seen on a visit back home. "Most of the fine old mansions have crumbled to dust with their owners," he said. So, good as Brigus is, it was bigger and better for the merchant class in the olden times.

Let us move quickly along to Holyrood (not pronounced hollyrude!) at the head of the bay (noting, however, that in Conception Harbour, along the way, there is an overfall which is well developed for swimming; it is in an area called The Pinch, and you can drive in for a dip and picnic); then head towards St. John's. You soon get into dormitory towns for the capital city, assembled in the large municipality called Conception Bay South. I intend no insult to such places as Foxtrap and Manuels and

Topsail by passing over them without extensive comment; they are now
essentially urban places, and since we are so close to St. John's, why not
get really urban and proceed to it? But let me note in passing that
Manuel's River is a wonderful site for a hike and possibly—for the
geologically minded—close study of trilobite fossils; while Topsail Beach,
though rough, is a favorite spot for many on a sunny summer's day. The
drive from Paradise, through St. Thomas and St. Phillip's, to Portugal
Cove, offers lovely views of the bay and Bell Island. Auntie Crae's Bakery
& Coffee Roastery on Old Broad Cove Road, open seven days a week until
9:00 p.m., sells hot homemade soups, fresh sandwiches, excellent
croissants, cakes, and bread, and the finest coffee on the peninsula.
Should you wend your way down to the beach at Beachy Cove, you will
find it to be a pleasant bucolic setting. There is a fine book called *The
Foxes of Beachy Cove*, written by Harold Horwood, which you can
sometimes pick up in second-hand bookstores. Try Afterwords Book
Store, 166 Water St., St. John's (753-4690).

St. John's

St. John's is, as earlier stated, the best Newfoundland has to offer to
tourists. The population of the urban region (including the city of Mount
Pearl, which is, in everything except legality, a part of St. John's) is
around 150,000. In the downtown, it is a quaint, perhaps somewhat dirty,
old harbor city; alas, the harbor isn't as busy as it once was, but part of
the pleasure here nonetheless is sitting on rocks on Signal Hill or at Fort
Amherst and watching boats go out and in through The Narrows. Try to
go out yourself; your hotel may arrange boat tours. If not, contact Action
Sail Tours (726-4011), which operates the 56-foot motor/sail tourboat
Annaville from St. John's harbour, or City & Outport Adventures
(747-8687). Or try the "Scademia," a schooner owned by Adventure Tours
Inc. (726-5000). Sailing out and in through The Narrows is an experience
you won't forget.

    Now, the bad news: the harbor regrettably receives raw sewage from
both St. John's and Mount Pearl, an unpleasant thought as you stroll
along the waterfront with your beau on a summer's evening.

    I have already said a lot about the city of St. John's in the course of
this *Guide*. May I now tell you what I think are ten of the best things to
see and do there (or in the immediate vicinity)? I shall assume you are
setting out from Hotel Newfoundland in the East End.

    You can get a free street map of St. John's put out by the municipal
council. This has a numbered index to places of note, plus information
on the back about parks, historic sites, buildings of interest, churches,
shops, attractions, etc. If you want a map before coming, write to City of

St. John's, Economic Development, Tourism Division, P.O. Box 908, St. John's, Nfld. A1C 5M2; phone 709-576-8106/8455. Ask as well for *Exploring the City of Legends*, a pamphlet with suggested walking tours, and another entitled *St. John's, Tourist Information Guide*—a very useful compendium. Regrettably, there is no book-length guide to St. John's. Jack A. White's *Streets of St. John's* has a lot of information. Bill Guihan's *Sketches of the Old City* has appealing drawings of old buildings, but I note that he misnames the National War Memorial the "Provincial" War Memorial, which suggests that he might be inaccurate in other things.

Be prepared to walk. The part of the old city that has most of what you will want to see—roughly from City Hall on New Gower Street east to Signal Hill, and from Harvey Road-Military Road south to the waterfront—is really quite compact; and there's precious little parking down there anyway, unless you want to use the Municipal Parking Garage on Water Street.

1. A walk on Water Street is essential. Not many years back, this street was where everyone shopped. It had big department stores, fish exporters, wholesale houses, outfitters for the fishery, etc. Most of these premises have vanished, but some of the old buildings remain. Start off in the little harbour-side park by the pilot dock (down from the National War Memorial). This is really a lovely little place. Immediately next to it is Gill's Cove. Walk down there, go to the right-hand corner (where boats are often tied up), and you have a perfect view of The Narrows, Signal Hill, and The Battery (the community under the hill). Turn around: you'll see you're standing in front of one of the harbour's leading lights (the lights mariners use to enter). The site gives a good sense of what a great harbour St. John's is. As you head west, you will find many intriguing shops and boutiques: The Olde Victorian Shoppe, for instance, at 100 Water St.; Wild Things, 124 Water St.; Newfoundland Weavery, 177 Water St.; the North West Company, 220 Water St.; and Nonia, 286 Water St. Just to mention five. Go as far west as the liquor store in the Murray Premises, 315 Water St., to replenish your supplies. There's a good place to eat lunch in the Murray Premises: it's in the store called Living Rooms.

2. Set out on a walk west along Duckworth Street, noting the poky little shops, the National War Memorial, the various lanes. Around here, the ambience of old St. John's can still be felt. The Cod Jigger, 245 Duckworth St., is a good place to buy Newfoundland crafts, jewelry, sweaters, etc.; the Stone Garden Gallery (same address) has sculptures by Nathaniel Noel, made from the mineral pyrophyllite, which is mined at Manuels. Go on to Church Hill, stopping off on the way to visit the Newfoundland Museum. Look at the Court House as well. On Church Hill, visit the Anglican Cathedral, consecrated in 1850, based on a design obtained from the English architect Sir George Gilbert Scott. Walk back

along Gower Street to Cochrane Street; note the architecture and colors of the houses, packed together. Go up the hill to Military Road. Have a look at St. Thomas's Church on the way back to the Hotel bar. Throughout this route, keep an eye out for monuments.

3. Go back up Military Road, past St. Thomas's Church, Government House (home of the Lieutenant-Governor), the elegant Colonial Building (which once housed both the Assembly and Legislative Council—go in and have a look), through Rawlins Cross, to the Roman Catholic Basilica of St. John the Baptist, which you must visit. (Perhaps walk through Bannerman Park on your way, looking around the perimeter to where people with money live, or used to live.) You will see a plaque to Governor John Harvey near the Basilica, though what he did to deserve one remains in doubt. Go west until you come to the beginning of Freshwater Road: a region famous for fish and chips shops, now rebuilding after a big fire. Walk down Longs Hill, Church Hill, and McBride's Hill to Water Street.

4. By now you have seen such architectural splendor as St. John's offers. If you want to see it from a distance, take a cab to the south side of the harbor, and get out just before the Irving Oil terminal. Now you can see the old city as a panorama. The Basilica dominates the view, of course. Near it on the left—your left—is St. Bon's College, once *the* place for the education of Roman Catholic boys. See that smokestack without smoke on the right? That building used to be the Imperial Tobacco Company, which within living memory manufactured such brands as Target, Bugler, and Royal Blend. Once that closed, manufacturing in St. John's was dealt a severe blow, though ice-cream, margarine, paint, and a few other odds and ends are still made here. Note the tall red and greenish spire of the Kirk sticking up over the horizon on the left of the Basilica; the reddish Gower Street United Church is below the Basilica on the left, as is the Anglican Cathedral. Immediately below the Basilica is the Benevolent Irish Society; to the right is the old Seventh Day Adventist church, now remade into condos (blue, wooden); down and to the left of the condos is the Masonic Temple (red, imposing); you can see the Court House just in front of that. On the far right you will catch the black spire of St. Thomas's Church. The Byzantine-looking roof on the right belongs to Cochrane Street United Church. Along Water Street, you will see the squat brown parking garage and a couple of "skyscrapers." To the right on Water Street is the red George V Institute, where the frozen bodies of the sealers of the *Newfoundland* were taken to be thawed in the spring of 1914. Seventy-seven men perished in that disaster.

5. Now that you are over on the South Side, you can do a number of interesting things. You have already passed a monument set in a kind of meadow south of the road: that marks the site of the old Anglican church of St. Mary the Virgin, beloved of seamen; near it the last Beothuck, Shanadithit, was buried. (The exact spot is unknown.) Near

that spot is the CN Dockyard, an industry well supported over the years from the public purse. Walk east of the Irving pier to the boat basin at Prosser's Rock, where you may well find fishermen at work. St. John's started out as a fishing station, and in a couple of places still is one. Go out to Fort Amherst, where you will see a lighthouse, concrete fortifications, now crumbling, built to keep the sneaky German U-boats at bay, and a magnificent view of Signal Hill opposite and of The Narrows. Want a real adventure? Near Fort Amherst there is a concrete pillar on the hill side of the road, covered with markings from highly literate passers-by. That pillar marks the beginning of a path up the South Side Hills—a steep, rocky path, not for the weary or sickly! If you take it, and keep going to the summit, you will find much to occupy you: paths, ponds, waterworks, and views of land and sea. It is perfectly possible to walk along the hill to Shea Heights.

6. Back to Hotel Newfoundland. Walk south of the hotel entrance to Devon Row—a line of houses that survived the catastrophic fire of 1892. Walk on to the Battery and explore this peculiarity—a fishing village on the fringe of the city; find your way to the path that leads into Signal Hill National Historic Park. That path leads right up to the top of the hill along the cliff face. It is safe, but arduous. If you're tired, don't walk up; take a cab to the top of Signal Hill and walk down. At any rate, don't miss this walk. There are other walks on or near the top of the hill, leading down towards Quidi Vidi village (usually pronounced kiddy viddy). Signal Hill National Historic Park is one of the glories of Newfoundland.

7. Walk around Quidi Vidi Lake and through the village itself. The path around the lake is now partly a boardwalk; very comfortable. Those white buildings on the north of the lake were part of the old U.S. Fort Pepperrell, an army base built during World War II. Those funny-looking buildings off to the east of the lake, up the hill? Those are the headquarters of the Federal Department of Fisheries and Oceans, on the White Hills. In those offices, weighty bureaucratic decisions are made to conserve and manage the fish resources off Newfoundland. And what a job they've made of it! Quidi Vidi village is scenic and intriguing. Want to walk farther? The hiking trail in fact goes through the east end of the city, along Rennies River all the way up to Long Pond—on the south and west of which are great places for birdwatching. On the north side of Long Pond is that Freshwater Resource Centre (phone 754-3474) I alluded to earlier. This is a "fluvarium"—the only one, I gather, in North America—where you can watch a stream flow by behind glass and see trout, etc. There is an entry fee: adults $2.75, small children, $1.50.

8. Drive to Cape Spear south of St. John's, the most easterly point in North America and a National Historic Site. Wave action on the rocks here can be spectacular; don't let the kids get too close. Or the dog! The old lighthouse of 1835 has been nicely restored. There is a great hiking

trail extending south along the coast where, from time to time, you will see a family of foxes. On the road out to Cape Spear, you can turn off to Maddox Cove and Petty Harbour, the latter a busy spot and a great place to knock around for a few hours.

9. North of the city lies a string of villages, among them Logy Bay, Middle Cove, Torbay, Flat Rock, and Pouch Cove. A leisurely drive along this shoreline will provide much to stimulate you, including an Ocean Sciences Centre at Logy Bay (phone 737-3706/3708). This is a part of Memorial University of Newfoundland. During the tourist season, i.e., from mid-June to September 1, from 10 a.m. to 6 p.m., seven days a week, visitors to the Centre are taken on tours by a guide (last tour starts at 5 p.m.). You will see (and be told about) seals and fish. There is a charge for the tour: $2.50 for adults, $1.50 for children. Middle Cove for its part has a nice rocky beach—a good spot for picnicking. Cape St. Francis, on the tip of the NE Avalon peninsula, has a lighthouse of course, and arresting views of the surrounding ocean. Another university facility of interest to tourists is the Oxen Pond Botanical Garden (737-8590), off Mount Scio Road north of the city. This is the Newfoundland equivalent of London's Kew Gardens—not quite as spectacular (you're in the colonies, my dear chaps), but beautiful nonetheless, with displays of various plants and flowers. It is open from 10 a.m. to 5:30 p.m., Wednesday to Sunday, from May 1 to November 30. Admission is free.

10. In front of Confederation Building, the location of most provincial government offices, are a number of sculptures and monuments. It is a good place to spend a couple of hours; there are visitors' parking spaces in front, the central foyer of the building has various displays of interest, and should you feel dazzled at being so near the seat of power you'll be able to sit and have a cup of coffee in a cafeteria. On the left of the building, as you face it, is the monument to the victims of the *Ocean Ranger* tragedy. The *Ocean Ranger* was an allegedly unsinkable semi-submersible oil rig that sank during a storm in the early morning of February 15, 1982, taking 84 men to their doom. There were no survivors. This was a bitter moment in a province that was beginning to think of itself as another Alberta. The monument reads: "In memoriam of those who lost their lives in the sinking of 'The Ocean Ranger' February 15, 1982." The names of all the men are listed. If somebody belonging to me had been lost in the disaster, I would not wish his name to appear under such an ignorantly-worded inscription.

Still in St. John's? Want to go to the movies? The Avalon Mall Cinemas (phone 726-9555) or Topsail Cinemas (364-8527) will accommodate you. The best park in the city is Bowring Park in the west end. This has an outdoor swimming pool for children (often overcrowded, however) and a number of statues, one of which, the Fighting Newfoundlander, shows a soldier heaving a grenade towards the Waterford Hospital. If you want to ignore all my advice and have someone give you a guided tour, phone McCarthy's Party (781-2244), which, for $25 per person, June 1 to Sept. 1, will take you through St. John's and environs in a comfortable 12-passenger van; or call City & Outport Adventures (747-8687).

The Southern Shore

The coast south of St. John's to Trepassey is called the Southern Shore. Politically, a lot of it belongs to the district of Ferryland, known in Newfoundland as the district where the option of Confederation with Canada received the least support in the referenda of 1948. In the first referendum, only 206 voters chose Canada; 3,364 were against it. Nowadays, however, you see some Canadian flags flying.

This is a shoreline of great beauty and interest though, since it is so close to St. John's, it is rapidly modernizing in its northerly stretches. Bay Bulls and Witless Bay are in some ways dormitory towns for the capital; yet they retain a lot of the old ways. The latter has a number of fine old houses, some kept up, some dilapidated. I am very fond of Witless Bay, especially Gallows Cove Road on the south side, which leads to a rocky beach with low cliffs and a long hiking trail along the cliff edge that is ideal for birdwatching and just enjoying the sights. Do seek it out: one of the drawbacks of route 10 is that it takes you away from the ocean, so that you must find sideroads off it

Old hearth, Witless Bay.

like this one to get to see the gorgeous seascapes. There is a nice craft shop on this road: Country Garden & Crafts (334-2483). (On Gus Carey's Road, which joins Gallows Cove Road, there is an old stone hearth, fairly well preserved, a great rarity.) The Captain's Table, a restaurant on the main highway just past Witless Bay, is a cut above most roadside restaurants.

Off Witless Bay and the coastline south of it are the Great, Green, and Gull Islands, which together constitute the Witless Bay Ecological Reserve. You are not to land on these islands, but tours can easily be arranged (try Gatherall's Sanctuary Boat Charters, 334-2887, or O'Brien's Bird Island Charters, 753-4850/334-2355, both operating out of Bay Bulls) that get you quite close to the seabirds: common and thick-billed murres, Atlantic puffins, and Leach's storm-petrels in great numbers, plus kittiwakes, razorbills, and black guillemots. The northern fulmar has also been sighted, though I have yet to see one there. Whales tend to sport in this area. Mid-June to the end of July—the caplin season, or what used to be the caplin season before the wise men in the White Hills got their paws on that species too—is the best time to go out and look. You can look from the shore too, especially from that path at the end of Gallows Cove Road.

A little further south is Mobile, where it is alleged a goat once spoke to a certain Mr. Dillon. This gentlemen was quietly harvesting his potatoes one sunny fall day when, nearing a fence next to common ground, he heard someone say clearly: "You're diggin' 'em, Dillon." Looking up from his labors, Mr. Dillon saw only a goat peering, somewhat intently, at him through the fence. "Yes, I'm diggin' 'em, you son of a b——h," he replied, "but damned the one of 'em you're gettin'!" Whereupon the goat strolled off. (There are many versions of Dillon's reply, but what the goat said has been well established.)

And that's all there is to the story of the Mobile goat.

Proceeding south, Tors Cove, Burnt Cove, Bauline, and, beyond La Manche provincial park, Brigus South, are lovely communities that you should take time to visit; you have to go off route 10 to get to them. A kilometer or so past the entrance to La Manche park, there is a road allegedly going to La Manche itself. Do take this road to the end, where you will find a parking area and a marked trail to the right. After a twenty minute walk on this trail, you come to the site of the old community of La Manche, now vacated. It is one of the most striking settings I know: a deep indentation in the rocks, heavily wooded, with ledges on the cliffside where houses and stages were built. Clamber down the path to get the full flavor. (Some make their way to the other side: I wouldn't advise trying it.)

A couple of kilometers after the Brigus South turnoff, well before you come to Cape Broyle, there is a road to the right, Horse Chops Road. This leads to the 1,000-square-kilometer Avalon Wilderness Area, one of a number of places in the province, apart from national and provincial parks, where the wilderness is, to a degree, protected from human interference and industrial development. While hunting and fishing (in season) are permitted in the Avalon Wilderness area, and of course canoeing, camping, berry-picking, cross-country skiing, etc., cabins are forbidden and ATVs and snowmobiles are permitted only on existing roads. Thus this place does not attract the weekend partying types; it does attract people genuinely interested in wilderness experience.

If you want to go in, Horse Chops Road offers the readiest access (though there are other roads and trails leading into it). Both residents of Newfoundland and visitors must have a permit to go in: write to the Parks Division of the provincial Department of Tourism and Culture (address given on page 29; phone 729-2424), or call at the office of the Division on the second floor of the West Block of Confederation Building, St. John's. Get a *Users' Guide* (free) to the area at the same office; this has all the rules and regulations printed in it, details about access routes and a canoe route, and a large map which should be sufficient for most visitors. If you want to have more detailed information about the terrain, buy these topographical maps: "Bay Bulls," "St. Catherine's," and "Holyrood" (for the address, see page 41). You should have a good 4-wheel drive vehicle with a high clearance—the roads are primitive—and of course a canoe. Be prepared to rough it. (My advice is to have this trip well planned before your arrival on the island.)

Now you can wander into the heart of the Avalon Wilderness Area. After you go past the dam and water supply area for Cape Broyle, you come to a fork in the road. As you will see on the map, the right fork will take you to Franks Pond—deep in the wilderness. What is in here? A caribou herd; moose; other animals; excellent fishing; splendid scenery. It is mostly barren ground, with ridges, tucks of woods, some high hills. Very peaceful and remote.

I know a licensed guide who might be prepared to take you in the Avalon Wilderness Area: Ben Dunne, 11 Smallwood Drive, Mount Pearl, Nfld. The area is his specialty.

But back to the main road. Ahead of you are the six main communities of the lower Southern Shore: Cape Broyle, Calvert, Ferryland, Aquaforte, Fermeuse, and Renews. I once spent many pleasant days canvassing in these places, asking for votes for a political candidate who, despite having outharbor roots, did not win the people's favor. They preferred a horny-handed son of toil by the name of John Crosbie. I haven't often mentioned museums in this *Guide*, but the one at Ferryland is strongly recommended. George Calvert, later Lord Baltimore, established a colony at Ferryland in 1621, overwintered there with his family in 1628-9, found it much too cold for his liking, and abandoned it for the more congenial climate of Maryland. Ferryland is strongly conscious of its antiquity. It has also produced some fine artists and craftspeople. Ferryland hooked mats are well known, as are the folksy but endearing paintings of the late Arch Williams. The land- and seascapes in the vicinity were painted in the 1970s by Gerald Squires, who lived with his family in the Ferryland lighthouse, in a series called "The Ferryland Downs."

But perhaps the place I like best in this cluster of settlements is Port Kirwan, on the north side of Fermeuse Harbour—an exquisite setting which the artist Don Wright made his home.

Where to stay in this area? Gatherall's in Bay Bulls, already mentioned, is a hospitality home as well as a touring business ($38 single, $48 double). But as I've said, I like sleeping in a tent; and there happens to be a great park beyond Cappahayden to the south, Chance

Cove Provincial Park, ideal for camping. It is a big park, distant from communities, unsupervised, and the camping area, near the ocean, is well off route 10 on a dirt road; thus it is usually uncrowded. There's no fee for camping here. My tent has on occasion been the only one in the park. To add to this, Chance Cove is a terrific place for walking, swimming, and beachcombing.

Beyond Cappahayden the terrain soon flattens into the characteristic marshes of the southern Avalon. Those who have an interest in paleontology may wish to take the 16 km drive from Portugal Cove South to Mistaken Point Ecological Reserve, where fossils of 600 million-year-old multicelled organisms—about twenty different kinds of animals, once living on a deep floor in the ocean—have been found. These are among the earliest such organisms ever recorded. You can drive to Long Beach on a rough road, then find your way to the protected area, which is extensive. Digging is prohibited. This searching for fossils is for the cognoscenti; ordinary folk might not know what to look for once they get there.

Trepassey, whose FPI fishplant once made it the hub of the southeast Avalon, faces an uncertain future now that FPI has lost interest in the town. It is a big community with many services of use to tourists. I have stayed here, and found enough to make me want to stay longer. Having left Trepassey, take the paved road south to St. Shotts, a fishing community in a setting so harborless and exposed that boats are pulled ashore each day for safekeeping—an uncommon procedure in Newfoundland, hard on men and boats. Watching cod being landed at St. Shotts is a remarkable sight. I wonder if we will ever see it again.

Heading along the flat bog stretching west from Trepassey, you inevitably see caribou from the Avalon herd, so keep your camera ready. If it is foggy, a not unknown phenomenon in these parts, proceed cautiously.

Towards Placentia

Peter's River is where you hit beautiful St. Mary's Bay. You may wish to linger here for a day or two. At St. Vincent's you cross the gut of Holyrood Pond, a long body of salty water where there used to be good fishing—even cod-jigging in winter through the ice. It is ideal for boating; a touch loppy for canoeists. Holyrood Pond provincial park may tempt campers, though the last time I was there loud music from nearby rock-freaks interrupted the birdsongs.

The highway north (route 90) to St. Catherine's offers occasional breathtaking views of the bay. Try to get off the main road to out-of-the-way places: the tiny community of Mall Bay, for instance, or

Admiral's Beach, a modern little town with the old section down near the beach, from which I have fond memories of good times. Salmonier Arm, farther along, is a delight to look at, while Salmonier River is, as old Prowse said, "a capital river for sport." If you have youngsters fussing in the back seat, you might now wish to go straight on along 90 to the Salmonier Nature Park (229-7888), open from noon to 8 p.m., Thursday to Monday (the main gate actually closes at 7 p.m.), where you can view a lot of the animals found in the province—some of them, such as the lynx and peregrine falcon, rarely seen—in a setting that is both congenial and natural. Admission is free. Its season is from the first Thursday in June to the Labor Day weekend.

Back to the head of the bay. Take the road through Mount Carmel and Harricott to Colinet. The peaceful village of Harricott was one of the places on the island (some others are Markland, near Whitbourne, Brown's Arm, near Lewisporte, and Cormack, near Deer Lake) where the well-intentioned Commission of Government in the 1930s tried to establish "land settlements"—i.e., farming communities. Families were moved here and elsewhere and given land, in the hope that Newfoundland eventually would reduce its dependence on fish. Such was the fantastic policy of an earlier time—that Newfoundlanders, as well situated as any people on earth to exploit the fisheries, should instead try to scratch a living from the soil! Not that farming cannot be successfully carried out in parts of the island; but even Prowse conceded that Newfoundland "does not have the soil of Manitoba," and to downgrade the importance of fishing is a policy of despair, if not madness. The history of Newfoundland industrial development is filled with crazy schemes such as manufacturing chocolate and rubber, driving Dogies down the Burin peninsula, setting up elaborate resort hotels in remote spruce groves, and growing cucumbers in acre-wide greenhouses. Fishing was our real chance; and we may have blown it.

There being no liveyers on the coast between North Harbour and Branch, the dirt road (route 92) strays far from the coast so that you see only bog, trees, and barrens, of which by this time you may have had a bellyful. But the road does cross rivers good for fishing; and in a few places you can, with effort, find your way to the seacoast for, say, camping or picnicking. The marshes to the west are good for bakeapples. I know outdoorsmen who prefer this lonely, bleak coast to any other on the Avalon.

At Branch you come to the usual southern flatlands. Branch is known for its fishermen. I have heard it said they are the best in Newfoundland, and have no reason to doubt it, though their proximity to the once bounteous inshore fishing grounds to the south and west might be thought to give them an advantage. Those grounds are the subject of one of Newfoundland's best-loved songs, the melancholy "Let me fish off Cape St. Mary's," by Otto Kelland. The harbor here is a makeshift, muddy affair, and to land in it when there's a lop on takes considerable skill and knowledge of wave patterns. Even for veteran boatmen, it is a perilous undertaking.

South of Branch is Point Lance, settled by the Irish in the early 19th century mainly as a farming community. Its spaciousness, so unlike many coastal communities huddled against cliffs, gives it the look of farmland, and the soil is fertile by local standards. Though tiny, Point Lance has had a book written about it, John Mannion's *Point Lance in Transition*, a splendid short work by an Irish geographer who, luckily for us, has made Newfoundland his home. I would not want you to travel on this remote peninsula without seeing Point Lance—as remarkable as its sister community across St. Mary's Bay, St. Shotts.

The next place you *must* see. It is the famed Cape St. Mary's bird sanctuary, about 15 km off the highway between Branch and St. Bride's. The access road is now paved. For sheer spectacle, there is nothing like this on the island. On arriving at the headquarters, you must walk for 20 to 25 minutes to get near what is called Bird Rock, a seastack that is the main nesting site. This is smothered with gannets, shrieking, landing, taking off from the sides or top of the cliff. You can get really close to the birds here, which of course is thrilling. There is no doubt that the specialty of this sanctuary is the gannet: it is alleged that there is but one gannetry larger than this in North America. Approaching Bird Rock along the very high cliffs, you see gannets flying above and below you, their wings beautifully tipped with black. But here as well along the cliffs are murres and kittiwakes in abundance, plus a small group of razorbills, and other species. The razorbill auk is said to be the closest surviving relative of the extinct great auk.

It is cold on Cape St. Mary's. Dress warmly; wear good walking boots.

Now, west to St. Bride's, where you will find places to put you up if you want to spend another day—or longer, if you're a birdwatcher—at the Cape, then north along what is called the Cape Shore to Point Verde. This is a coast of steep hills and deep valleys, scary and entrancing, offering on occasion something close to a Disneyland rollercoaster ride. The newly-paved road is high up; Placentia Bay stretches gloriously to the west. Very few people live in the coves. Gooseberry Cove and Ship Cove are very striking places; you come towards them from high hills, so that they are seen from above, like an Alpine village. There is a provincial park (no camping) at the former; off Ship Cove, President F.D. Roosevelt met Prime Minister Winston Churchill in August, 1941, a meeting that resulted in the Atlantic Charter (note the monument here). Once seen, the Cape Shore is not quickly forgotten.

At Placentia or Dunville, find a motel and wait for the Argentia ferry. This is a good place to spend a day or two. A big U.S. naval base was built at Argentia during World War II; a whole community, including a graveyard, had to be removed to accommodate the Americans. Castle

Hill National Historic Park will appeal especially to Francophone visitors, for it is the site of French forts built in the 17th and 18th centuries. Placentia itself, a town built on a beach, is intriguing. Fox Harbour and Ship Harbour are well worth the time spent getting to them.

A few more travel hints

Don't come to Newfoundland from a foreign country expecting the medicare plan here to look after you if you get sick. Buy health insurance. If you have no such insurance, you will be billed for the services provided. Don't try to take fresh produce out of the province; Canada Customs officials will seize it as you get on the ferry. Learn the other customs regulations that apply to you.

In addition to customs regulations, the Government of Newfoundland has restrictions on inter-provincial movement of liquor and cigarettes. A visitor from, say, Nova Scotia is permitted to bring to Newfoundland the following: one carton of cigarettes, one 40-oz bottle of liquor, nine litres of wine, and 24 bottles of beer. If you want to bring in more than this, you must get permits prior to coming, and arrange to pay provincial sales taxes. Have gravol with you when you get on the ferry; the crossings can be rough.

Gifts to take back with you

If you have a good bit of money to spare, buy Newfoundland art; it's the best bargain around. See the names of artists given earlier, page 35.

Books. The *Dictionary of Newfoundland English*, by G.M. Story, W. Kirwin, and J.D.A. Widdowson; Cassie Brown, *Death on the Ice* (sealing disaster of 1914); *The Prints of Christopher Pratt 1958-1991* (Newfoundland's finest artist); *In the Good Old Days*! by P.K. Devine (nostalgic reminiscences); *Mary Pratt* (with excellent plates of her paintings); *The Danger Tree*, by David Macfarlane; *Part of the Main*, by Peter Neary and Patrick O'Flaherty (a modestly priced illustrated history of Newfoundland); *This Marvellous Terrible Place*, by Yva Momatiuk and John Eastcott (wonderful photos; fine text); *The Story of Bobby O'Malley* or *The Divine Ryans* by Wayne Johnston (comic novels); *House of Hate*, by Percy Janes (classic Newfoundland novel); *The Shipping News*, by E. Annie Proulx (set in Newfoundland; award-winning American novel); *Newfoundland in the North Atlantic World, 1929-1949*, by Peter Neary (of special interest to American visitors, since it deals with U.S. bases in Newfoundland during World War II); *Ray Guy's Best*, by Ray Guy (satiric and nostalgic columns); Dennis Minty, *Wildland Visions* (lovely photos); *Atlas of Newfoundland and Labrador* (a fine work); *Canada's Incredible Coasts* (National Geographic publication; good writing on Newfoundland; brilliant photos); Cabot Martin, *No Fish and Our Lives* (the fish crisis); Thomas Dawe, *In Hardy Country* (poems); *The Plays of CODCO*, ed. Helen Peters.

Music. CDs and/or cassettes: "All the Best: Folk Music of St. John's" (great songs by a number of artists); "Figgy Duff" (there are later recordings also by this group, but this is possibly the best); "Another Time: The Songs of Newfoundland" (another fine collection by various performers); "Humouring the Tunes," by the late Rufus Guinchard (Newfoundland's greatest fiddler); "The Brule Boys in Paris," Tickle Harbour; "The Colour of Amber," Anita Best & Pamela Morgan (love songs); Buddy Wassisname and the Other Fellers (a number of titles available; you can't miss); Colcannon; "January," Mary Barry; "Different Paths," Shirley Montague; The Irish Descendants; Great Big Sea.

Miscellaneous. Mitts and coats made from Grenfell cloth; knitted goods (mitts, sweaters, hats, etc.); woven goods (sweaters, scarves, place mats, etc.); locally made jewelry; sealskin products (cheap, very good buy); foodstuffs (bottled savoury, jams, tinned sealmeat, etc.); pink, white, and green flags; Newman's Port; silver pitcher plant brooch (ask at a jeweler's); pitcher plant cup and saucer set.